# *Make Room*

# *For Jesus*

# *In Your Inn*

*By*

*Gwendolyn Adele Bancroft*

PEARSON-SCHLEE PUBLISHER

EDITED BY EDWIN E. PRONG

PHOTOS: DAVID TIMOTHY PRONG

ILLUSTRATIONS: KAREN SAGE

# Author, Gwendolyn Bancroft

**MAKE ROOM FOR JESUS IN YOUR INN**

**Make Christmas exciting with Jesus !**

**COPYRIGHT @ 1999**

**GWENDOLYN BANCROFT**

ISBN: 0-7392-0460-2

Library of Congress Catalog Card Number: 99-96535

Printed in the U.S.A. by

Morris Publishing

3212 E. Hwy 30 • Kearney, NE 68847 • 1-800-650-7888

## DEDICATION

I dedicate this book to our granddaughter, Megan, who has helped with the story since she was two years old. Megan wanted to hear the story over and over. When asked what Mary brought to the temple, she'd answer in her baby prattle,"twoturdovs". Of course, Grandma knew it was "two turtle doves".

When Megan was three, the Kiwanis of Traverse City had invited me to speak early one morning. I decided to take only the Temple figures with me. When I returned, Megan was getting up and wanted to hear the story. Then she noticed figures were missing. She asked "Where's Simeon and Anna?" We have six hundred pieces and she missed the two I had left in my car!

At four, Megan asked if she could give the next tour. I agreed since just friends were coming over. I knew they would enjoy her version of the story. She said, "The angel came to Zachariah, and told him his daughter was going to have a baby." Megan corrected herself, " No.....his wife"! Then she continued calmly, " Zachariah did not believe him so the angel said he would not be able to talk for nine years. No......nine months! Then the angel told Mary she was going to have a baby." Megan held her hands to her face and yelled, "OH, NO"! Knowing I was her role model, I chuckled while observing how she was retelling the story.

Megan is eight now and has asked to have the large six hundred piece set when she gets older. Therefore, I dedicate this book to the tour guide of the future, Megan Adele Hawley, my granddaughter, who has my middle name, as well as my heart. May the Holy Spirit guide her words and the angels watch over her as she tells this most wonderful and awesome story in the world today. The story of our Savior's birth.

Love, Grandma Gwen

3

# TABLE OF CONTENTS

FOREWORD..................................................................................................6

INTRODUCTION.........................................................................................8

ACKNOWLEDGMENTS..............................................................................10

CHAPTER 1   THROUGH THE EYES OF OUR  LITTLE ONES

Two, Three and Four-Year-Olds Meet Mary and Joseph......................................11

CHAPTER 2   JESUS SAID, " LET THE CHILDREN COME UNTO ME."

Five, Six and Seven-Year-Olds Meet Jesus Through Symbols ...........................26

CHAPTER 3   OUT OF THE MOUTHS OF BABES

Third through Seventh Graders learn a Christian Vocabulary............................37

CHAPTER 4 JESUS' MOTHER, A YOUNG TEEN AGER

Teens discover how the Old Testament relates to the Christmas Story. ................48

CHAPTER 5  JUST AS THE TREE WAS BENT, THE TREE INCLINED

Young Adults Learn to be Role Models................................................61

CHAPTER 6 AND THE WORD WAS MADE FLESH

Adults 55+ Perceive Seeing is Believing.................................................79

CHAPTER 7 GRANDPARENTS, TODAY'S WISE MEN

Customs of our Forefathers.................................................................90


CHAPTER 8 FROM NAZARETH TO EGYPT

Traveling with Mary and Joseph.........................................................104


CHAPTER 9 PROPHECIES IN THE CHRISTMAS STORY

Proof Jesus is the Messiah .................................................................110


CHAPTER 10  THE MEANING OF ADVENT

Jesus is Coming.................................................................................118


CHAPTER 11  CHRISTMAS EVE

"T'Was The Night Before Christ's Birth............................................132


CHAPTER 12  CHRISTMAS

The Twelve Days...............................................................................138


CHAPTER 13 EPIPHANY

Wise Men Bring Gifts.......................................................................150


CHAPTER 14  MESSENGERS FROM GOD

Angels We Have Heard on High.........................................................160


GLOSSARY........................................................................................164

# FOREWORD

## A JOURNEY TO FIND JESUS AT CHRISTMAS

Growing up, my sister and I only knew about Santa and the North Pole. This journey from the Santa materialism to God's gift in Bethlehem took many decades. Unlike the Wise Men we didn't have a star (or a role model) to follow to find Jesus in the Christmas story.

My first husband, Ed Prong, and I discussed what we could do about the commercialism of Christmas. We didn't know of any path to Bethlehem. However, we chose not to have Santa in our home. We decided not to start the myth. We felt when our son Keith found out there wasn't any Santa, he'd perceive that maybe God was a myth, too. We resolved to make it exciting and fun with audio-visual aids. We wanted only to tell the real Christmas story.

When our first-born was three years old, we bought figures of Mary, Joseph and Jesus for twenty-nine cents each. Putting Mary and Joseph on one side of the room and a shoe box for the stable at the other side, we let Keith move Mary and Joseph closer to the stable each day. On Christmas eve, he put them in the stable and we told him, if baby Jesus was in the manger in the morning he could open his presents. We kissed him good night and tucked him in bed. After Keith was asleep, we put baby Jesus in the manger.

At three A.M., we were awakened suddenly with Keith shaking us and saying, "Jesus is here, Jesus is here." How excited he was! At first, we were frightened thinking it was the Second Coming! Once we realized he had found Jesus in the manger, we smiled. We knew then, we were hooked on the enthusiasm Jesus brought to our child at Christmas.

6

Our son had taught us how exciting a Christmas with Jesus could really be. We knew we'd always want to go to Bethlehem for Christmas instead of the North Pole.  At this time, we still eagerly go there!

Now, after many decades, our family nativity set has more than six hundred pieces. We have added each figure to help the story become more alive. However, we have given away more figures than we have collected for our own Nativity set.  Every year, my husband Ken and I have over a hundred people take our "Bethlehem Tour."  It is our witness to the joy of Christ's birth. There is no charge.  We also give everyone who comes a souvenir and usually refreshments.  We have boy scouts, brownies, senior citizens, hospice and many church groups and Christian School classes, grandparents bringing little ones and we even had a family reunion and birthday party.  Children love to help us move the figures as we tell the story.

Best of all are the small groups of two or  three that come to hear the prophecies and after the tour sit around telling us of the peace they  found by hearing the story in a different way.  This book illustrates new ideas for giving Jesus more room in your "Inn."

# INTRODUCTION

Gwen Bancroft has been called the "Little People Lady" by many children because of the little Nativity figures she has given them over the years. In 1953, Gwen was a member of St. Augustine's Episcopal Church in Benton Harbor, Michigan. At Christmas each Sunday School child was given a box of candy featuring Santa Claus. Wanting to replace Santa with God's great Christmas gift of Jesus, Gwen offered to buy the gifts the following year.

At Christmas, 1954, Gwen gave each child a Nativity figure with which to start a Nativity set of their own. She continued giving different figures each year to the children, and over the course of thirty-four years, she has given away over 4,000 figures.

Gwen Adele Bancroft is a wife, mother, grandmother, and great grandmother. At the early age of nineteen, she started teaching in Monroe, Michigan. Later, in 1960, while teaching in the Benton Harbor (Mich.) Public Schools, Gwen wrote a Black History teacher's guide using creative methods for use with elementary children in Michigan. In the same year, she pioneered a program to help adult illiterates learn to read and write, using Frank Laubach's "Each One Teach One" approach. Traveling, about the state on weekends she gave birth to many more such programs. In 1970, she developed a Black History Pride program, an adaptive concept for use in the Grand Rapids, (Mich.) Public Schools.

For thirty years, Gwen was active in politics, both as an officer on the local level, and as a delegate to state and national conventions. After thirty-four years she retired from teaching, but not community life. An active volunteer, Gwen visits hospice patients, & nursing homes, tutors young children in reading, baby-sits and serves on church committees.

In 1991, Gwen and her husband Ken moved to Traverse City, Michigan the first week in Advent.  Not having their membership transferred yet to the local church, Gwen and Ken were delighted when the Pastor asked if the Senior Group could come to see their extensive Nativity sets.  It was then that a new tradition was started.  Gwen decided instead of giving Nativity figures to Sunday School children, she would give figures to people who toured their home and listened to the Christmas story.

For many years, during the Christmas season, tours have been given as a witness that it is Christ's birthday.  Facts about all facets of Jesus' birth are told in a great variety of ways in every room in their home. At the conclusion of a tour, tea and cookies are served and souvenirs given to guests, in honor of Jesus' birthday.  Gwen truly loves her Lord and delights in telling the Christmas story.  The witness of her love of Jesus comes through as she tells the story of the Old Testament prophesies and how they came true with the birth of Jesus, the Messiah, our Savior.

By  Shirley Halliday Rhodes
"The Angel Lady"

Author

Gwen  Bancroft

9

# ACKNOWLEDGMENTS

To our son, Keith Steven Prong, who started the whole thing, by yelling, "Jesus is here, Jesus is here!" more than four decades ago.

To my husband, Ken, who makes a cross stitch each year to illustrate the Jesus Story. Last year the hanging said, " Be not forgetful to entertain strangers: for thereby some have entertained angels unawares." Hebrews 13:2.

To our daughter, Brenda Kay Frarey, for the unique Advent, Christmas, and Epiphany sweat shirts she has made for us to wear during the tours.

To our daughter, Nancy Isabelle Mercier, who helps bake cookies for the tours. She is my special angel, lifting me by her presence and spirit.

To our son, David Timothy Prong who always finds special items; such as ethnic angels, a Jesse Tree, village people, King Herod and Caesar Augustus.

To our son, Steven Bancroft, for the Precious Moments' Nativity Set.

To our daughter, Kathy Sue Delcamp, for our Tiffany Nativity set.

To our daughter, Karen Sage, for our wooden set and a quilt nativity.

To my mentor, Shirley Brackett for the use of her computer ability and technical skills, friendship, patience and encouragement.

# CHAPTER 1

## CHRISTMAS THROUGH THE EYES OF LITTLE ONES
### Two, Three and Four-Year-olds Meet Mary and Joseph

What a delightful age to learn about Jesus' birth. Children at this age haven't yet become aware of all the commercialism of Christmas. They can be easily guided towards the real joy of the holy day. The ensuing instructions are to help form a tradition which is meaningful for your family. May your children learn about Jesus, Mary and Joseph. May your journey begin with your children knowing Christ is the important part of CHRISTmas and be excited about finding Jesus in the manger.

## PLANTING THE GOOD NEWS OF JESUS

How do we start a tradition where we make room for Jesus in our home instead of delegating His place to the stable? Have you wondered from where your parents' traditions of Christmas came? Christmas is like the parable in Mark 4: 2-9. We must plant the seed, which is the Good News of Jesus Christ, in good soil so it can grow and be passed on to future generations. We must start worthy traditions.

*A sower went out to sow. And as he sowed, some seed fell on the path and the birds came and ate it up..* Luke sows the seed of the wonderful birth of Christ. Commercialism at Christmas just eats up the story of His birth so that in many homes the seed is no more.

*Other seed fell on rocky ground, where it did not have much soil, and it sprang up quickly, since it had no depth of soil. And when the sun rose, it was scorched and since it had no root, it withered away.* Seed, which falls in homes where Jesus' birthday is barely mentioned, cannot take root so it withers away. There Christmas and faith have no depth.

*Other seed fell among thorns, and the thorns grew up and choked it, and it yielded no grain.* The seed, which falls among people who do not have time for the real story of Christmas, is choked and yields no honor to Jesus. Thorns thrive in places which make Santa very important and visible. These people believe gifts are the key to a joyous Christmas.

*Other seed fell into good soil and brought forth grain, growing up and increasing in yield.* Seed, which falls in the hearts of children who are taught about Jesus, brings forth a harvest for the next generation. These children love Jesus and want to follow in His path. They have fun, fellowship and joy at Christmas plus something else. They have a meaningful, spiritual life with Jesus, the greatest gift of all. The word is in their mouth and their heart. How do we plant the seed in our children's hearts? How do we make our soil more productive?

The following chapters give suggestions on how to plant the seed at different ages. The good soil will help the roots grow deep. It will bring forth a plant which will yield great fruit. The family needs to provide nutriments for growth. The devil can bring doubt and disease to our faith. The more room we make for Jesus, the more our plant will blossom. A family project on the First Sunday of Advent could be to plant wheat seeds. Water daily and on Christmas Eve put them by the manger to symbolize the coming of Christ, the bread of life.

Take an inventory of how you celebrate Christmas now. Then take the challenge to make the knowledge of Jesus grow in your inn

## FIRST WEEK IN ADVENT

SUNDAY: If you have an Advent wreath, light one candle. An Advent calendar can be used in place of the wreath, however, it's difficult to find a suitable one. Parents can show there are four weeks in Advent on a regular calendar and help the children understand why on each Sunday one more candle is lit. Explain when all four candles are burning, it means Jesus' birthday is just a few days away. In Advent it is a fitting tradition to read a part of the Christmas story each day. My granddaughter, Megan, had a predictable routine of wanting to hear the story from her Children's Bible before breakfast.

Make a figure of Mary and the angel. Read Luke 1:26-28. Have a child hold the angel by Mary and tell Mary, she is going to have a baby. Here, you can ask the children how they think Mary must have responded to this surprising announcement. Preschoolers always want to touch and move the figures. Therefore, they will enjoy making their own complete set. The paper patterns in this chapter can be made small enough to be finger puppets or large enough to stand alone. Young children enjoy learning to draw Mary's and the angel's face. With practice they can learn to color the clothes inside the lines of the pattern.

Teach the actions to the following finger play:

Look around Mary. [ Put hands to eyes.]

Stop sweeping Mary! [Move arms like sweeping.]

Put down your broom. [Bend down.]

Look there's an angel in your room. [Put hand to eyes].

Look around Mary. Open your eyes. [Open and shut eyes.]

Look there is a visitor with a surprise. [Give surprised look.]

13

To help the children remember the sequence of the Christmas story each day review the part they know then add something new.

Glue back together.

Note: Tracing paper may be used to copy patterns for only personal use .

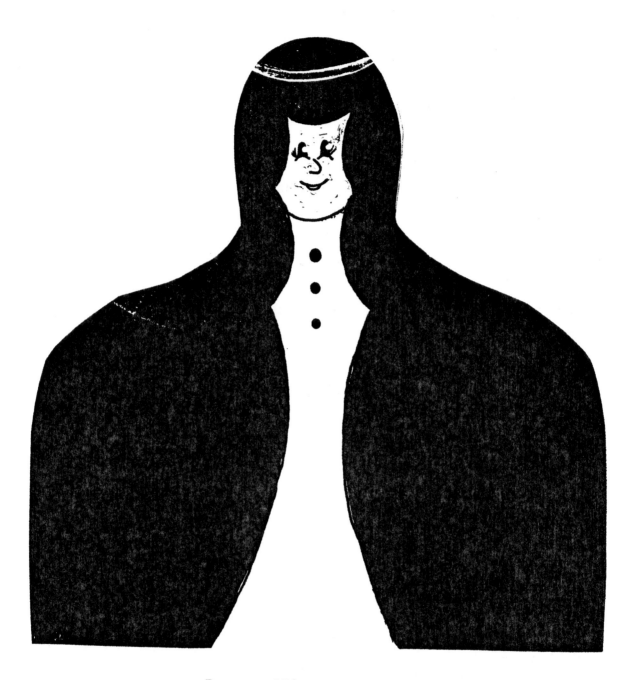

Pattern of Mary

MONDAY: Read Matthew 1: 20a and 21. Make a figure of Joseph. If you disclose the angel came to Joseph in a dream, your children might want to discuss their dreams. Some dreams, especially when they are chased by an animal, can make them feel vulnerable.

Teach hand actions to the following spoken by an angel to Joseph:

Listen to the angel Joseph. [Cup ear.]

God has need of you. [ Nod yes.]

Take good care of Mary, Joseph. [ Put arm around Mary.]

God has need of you. [ Nod.]

Choose a gentle donkey, Joseph. [ Brush donkey's coat.]

God has need of you. [Nod.]

You'll be in the Christmas Story. [ Point to him.]

You're important, too. [ Nod]

16

TUESDAY: Read Luke 2: 1-5a. Clarify why Mary and Joseph will need to go to Bethlehem to be counted. Have your children pretend to be census takers. Involve them in his job by counting books, people, chairs and tables.

WEDNESDAY:  Place a sign with "Bethlehem" on it in the southern part of the room. Discuss how and why people used inns. Make an inn out of a box.

THURSDAY: Use a library book to find caves used for stables. Discuss why animals stayed there. Make a stable out of a small box and put it by the inn.

FRIDAY: Make a manger out of a tiny box and place some hay in it.  Sing "Away in the Manger." Explain a manger is a feeding box for animals.

SATURDAY:  Clarify why Jesus' bed needs straw. Specify each time someone does a good deed, they may add a piece of straw to the manger. By making Jesus' bed soft, it's a way the children can say they love Jesus. Give examples of deeds right away, such as "You helped me make your bed, so you can put in a piece of straw," or "You told the story of Mary today, so you may put in a piece." They can use pieces of yarn or strips of paper to represent straw.

**SECOND WEEK IN ADVENT**

SUNDAY: Light two candles. Little ones do not have a sense of time. When it's their birthday, we wisely wait to remind them just a week in advance. However, since the stores are filled with Santa before Thanksgiving,  it is important the children know now whose birthday is really coming. Give each child their own calendar. Each Advent Sunday can be marked with a blue or purple crayon and Christmas Day marked in red.

Let them draw one candle in the space for last Sunday. Then have them cross off the previous six days. This will show them one week is already completed. Now draw two candles in the square for this Sunday. Tell them to cross off one square each day.

Explain Advent means "coming," and Jesus' birthday is coming. Challenge them to figure out how they can give gifts to Jesus. Their conclusion might be, they can give gifts to people who have Jesus in their heart. Ask how they know who has Jesus in their heart. Ask how they can show people they have Jesus in their heart? They will enjoy simple how and why questions.

MONDAY: Explain in Mary's time there weren't any buses or cars. Mary would have to ride a donkey or walk. Teach your child the fun of making a donkey sound. This is an excellent time to give a Christmas Story coloring book. The children can color all the donkeys in it. Make a donkey for their Nativity set.

TUESDAY: Discuss how long it would take to walk to another near-by town. Use a map in a Bible to show a route Joseph might have chosen. Place the figures of Mary and Joseph in the city of Nazareth in the north. Each day they need to be moved closer to Bethlehem. Our children's concept of south was down. Starting on the second floor, they would move the Holy Family down one step daily going southward. While rushing down the stairs one day, our daughter, Nancy, caused the donkey to fall down into a chasm. Her brothers jokingly said since the donkey broke it's leg, she'd have to take it to a vet. Nancy had heard her father was a vet (soldier) so she took the donkey to him. It turned out to be a wise decision. Her daddy glued the leg back.

WEDNESDAY: Make shepherds and put them in the hills of Judah (South end of room ). Tell the story of David, the brave shepherd. Have the children close their eyes and listen for sheep and the sound of a wolf coming out of the woods; then the sound of a sling shot going round and round and finally a cry and howl from the wolf as he is hit by a stone. Discuss how the shepherd's robe keeps the weather (sun, wind, sand) from bothering him. The children will love to dress up like a shepherd. Explain how Jesus our shepherd watches over us.

THURSDAY:   Explain the candy cane was made to help us remember the story of Christmas.  Find pictures of the shepherd's staff in the coloring book. Show how the shepherd used the hook to get a lamb out of a hole by hooking it around the lamb's body.  Show how it makes a "J" for Jesus when it's upside down.  Today, have the children tell the story about Mary and Joseph in their own words.  Explain every day they tell the story, their treat will be a candy cane to eat or add to the tree.  This will help them to memorize the story.

FRIDAY: Let your children make a lamb's pattern and on it paste cotton balls (to represent wool).  At this age they can use small glue bottles with skill.

SATURDAY:  Challenge your children to think of new ways to be helpful to earn straw, such as: by saying a prayer or putting napkins on the table.  Just puffing up a pillow after they help you make the bed should be enough for little children to earn straw.  It is important they feel useful.

**THIRD WEEK IN ADVENT**

SUNDAY: Light three candles.  In the Sunday square on the calendar draw three candles.  If Christmas cards have arrived, spread out the ones which tell about Jesus.  Make a game out of finding and placing pictures in the right sequence of events surrounding the birth of Jesus. First, find the card showing the Angel coming to Mary.  Next find Joseph.  Then baby Jesus sleeping in the manger.  Last find the lambs and shepherds in the field.  Then mix the cards up.  Let your children try to put them in the right sequence.  Each time you receive new cards they can play the game again.  Hide the Wise Men's cards until later.  They can learn to follow two- and three- step directions, to retell the story by analyzing the pictures.  Ask who's birthday is coming?

MONDAY: Paste a picture of Mary from a Christmas card on a sheet of paper. Beneath the picture write "Mary". On another sheet, paste a picture of Joseph and add his name. On a third sheet, paste an angel and add the word angel. Then staple the pages together and make a book. Don't use more then three different words until your children understand the concept of reading. Next week add more pages and two new words.

TUESDAY: Read Matthew 2:1-8. Your children will enjoy producing objects with scissors and by using them often will acquire some degree of skill. Let them make as many Wise Men as they wish and put them in the East.

WEDNESDAY: Read Matthew 2: 7-10. Mention the Wise Men knew Jesus was born because they saw a special star in the sky. Using a dipper to dish out soup, tell how they probably saw the big dipper in the sky as well. Let your children have fun in the dishwater or bathtub with dippers. Say they may stay up to see dippers in the sky some night. Use a constellation book to show how the stars form a big and small dipper. Help them draw a picture of one. Put stars on all the completed pages in the Christmas coloring book. With crayons let your child color the stars and then paint a blue sky over them.

THURSDAY: Make a list of wise people your children know (grandpa, grandma, dad, mom, minister and teachers ). Explain people learn through discovery and senses. Intellectually they can become smarter by learning about things. However, explain the most important way to grow is spiritually by hearing about Jesus and to know Jesus loves them and is their friend. They are part of God's family and should want to love and obey God.

FRIDAY: Make star cookies for Christmas Eve to put on the roof of the stable.

SATURDAY: Have your children make gift wrapping paper. Let them draw designs or buy an angel stamp to help with the project. Help your children to comprehend the time and love which goes into wrapping a gift.

## FOURTH WEEK IN ADVENT

SUNDAY: Light the fourth candle and tell how many days remain until Jesus' birthday. Help your children to use each day left to make a gift for someone. After each gift is made say, " Oh, I see you made a gift for someone who has Jesus in their heart." They can make a manger by pressing their thumb in a square of playdough. Make angel cookies for Daddy or grandma. Make swaddling clothes for dolls by stripping old pillow cases. They can cut Christmas cards into puzzles. For their Mom, they can finish Friday's book.

CHRISTMAS EVE: Make a birthday cake for Jesus. When the family arrives home from church, have someone play an innkeeper. Move Joseph and Mary to different inns. Have them knock to get in. Explain why some people will say "There is no room," and why they don't have room in their homes for Jesus. Explain some haven't heard the story of Jesus. Put Mary and Joseph in the stable where an innkeeper found a place for them. Check the straw in the manger. Tell your children, if they find Jesus in the manger in the morning, to wake you because it's time to open presents. Read 'TWas The Night Before Christ's Birth", found in Chapter 11.

## TWELVE DAYS OF CHRISTMAS :

CHRISTMAS DAY: Your children will be excited to see the tree if you put it up after they go to bed. It will be an extra gift for them. The tree probably will last the twelve days of Christmas if it is put up Christmas Eve. Have the children check the manger for Jesus.

If Jesus isn't there, they will have to go back to bed for awhile. When Jesus is there, ask who will get Jesus' birthday gifts. Then ask why. After your children open their first gift, they should watch while others open their first gift. As a gift is received, each person should reaffirm "Someone knows I love Jesus, I have a gift." Be sure to be a good role model. Give a hug to your children for the gift they made you. No one should open a second gift until everyone has opened one. It helps the children remember from whom they received the gift. Later, the children can blow out the candles on Jesus' cake and sing "Happy Birthday Dear Jesus" or they can act out the following:

The earth [touch the ground]

and the stars [reach up high]

All of the world [make a circle]

felt like a party that Christmas morn [clap hands once, lift them high and swing them apart].

God lit the lights [open and close both hands twice].

God sent the songs [cup hands and mouth-then extend hands].

God gave the present when His Son was born [clap as before].


Dec.26th: Have a child carry an angel to the shepherds and tell them to go to Bethlehem to see Baby Jesus wrapped in swaddling clothes lying in a manger.


Dec.27th: Have your children move the shepherds to the stable.


Dec. 28th: Children should accept the responsibility for making thank you cards. Send a picture of your child with the gift and your child's signature. At this age, their name is sometimes sufficient.

23

Dec. 29th: Have your children move them back to the hillside in Judah.

Dec.30th: Listen to your children tell the Christmas story. They are reflections of you.

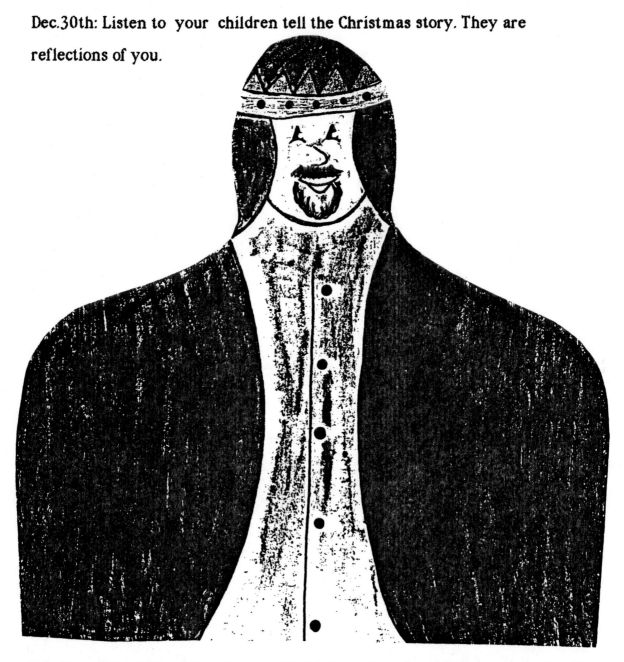

Dec.31st: Move Wise Men closer to Bethlehem. Let the children pretend to be riding the camels. What a bumpy ride! Read Matthew 2: 1-2. Let your children wear flowing robes, a scarf on their head and rings on their fingers, so they can pretend to be Wise Men.

24

Jan. 1st: Read Luke 2:21. On the 8th day , Jesus received His name. Explain why you gave your children their Christian names.

Jan. 2nd: Read Matthew 2: 3-9. Move Wise Men closer. Tell your children they can find a star inside an apple. Then cut one horizontal with the stem part on the top. When you cut it crosswise, you will see the seeds form a star.

Jan.3rd :Ask your children what four figures they would like next year. Explain, they may get one each Sunday in Advent. This helps the children decide which figures they'd use and enjoy the most. This gives you a year to find the ones they want on sale. Many little children want animals (a lamb, a cow, donkey or camel). Keep the set they made even if you buy one.

Jan. 4th: Inform by reading Matthew 11, the Wise Men found Jesus in a house. He was no longer in the stable. He was now a young child. Ask if they want to make a house for the Holy Family out of a box.

Jan. 5th: Announce this is the 12th and last day of Christmas. Describe all the jobs needed to be done tomorrow, which marks the end of Christmas.

EPIPHANY: Jan. 6th Read Matthew 2: 9-12. Move the Wise Men to the house with the Holy Family inside. Cut a piece of gold off a Christmas card to place it before Jesus. Some churches celebrate Jesus's birth on this day. Ask your children if they know their birth date. Ask if they would like a Child's Bible with colorful illustrations for their birthday. Assure your children your family will always have room for Jesus. Don't be surprised if they want to keep their Nativity set in their room. It is a comfort to many little ones.

# CHAPTER 2

## JESUS SAID "LET THE LITTLE ONES COME UNTO ME"
## Five, Six and Seven-Year-Olds Learn With Symbols

Children learn in multi-sensory ways: visual, audio and kinesthetic. Some children can master a subject by just one method. Others learn by using more than one. Symbols are important because they can be used in all three methods. Audio children will learn best by hearing about the symbols. The kinesthetic will learn by touching them and visual children learn by seeing symbols. At this grade level, children are learning how symbols (such as +, -, and =) have meanings. Through phonics they learn letters are symbols for sounds. In church, they learn many Biblical names are symbols for prophecies. Jesus' name means "He will deliver His people from their sins." David means "Beloved." This chapter will help your children discover the Christmas Story though the use of symbols in the home. For a better foundation, if you didn't have this book last year, you may want to start your children in Chapter One. It will help them learn how to set up and move their Nativity figures.

### FIRST WEEK IN ADVENT

SUNDAY: An **Advent wreath** can be made by putting a wreath around four candle sticks. Help your children learn a spiritual language. Explain that Advent means "coming." It's the time we prepare our hearts and minds for Jesus. The wreath is a circle reminding us God has no beginning and no end. God is always with us, in the bright day and the dark of night. The kinesthetic child will enjoy making the wreath or tying it together. There are **four candles** in an Advent Wreath to **symbolize the four weeks** in Advent. Light one candle. Name it Mary since she is very important this week.

If your children's paper set, made last year, needs replacing let your children use the same patterns. Then glue, staple or paper clip them to toilet paper rolls. They will last longer with this support. This added step is geared for this age level. Expose your children to a new symbol, daily in Advent. The following day review the meaning and usage of it to develop a logical system of remembering.

MONDAY: While you read Luke 1:26b-27 have your child hold an angel facing Mary. Ask your children why **angels** are symbols of Christmas. Children like to answer easy questions. Remind them how an angel named Gabriel came to Mary. He told her she was going to have a baby named Jesus. Tell the children most angels act as **messengers** for God. Find a picture of one.

**Your children's attention span will lengthen if you review the old symbols and add new ones daily until the lists becomes longer and longer. The routine helps them to accurately predict what the reply should be. The \* is to remind you to review something each day.**

TUESDAY: \* Read Luke 1:28. Have your children draw **halos** above the heads of angels. Explain halos give the illusion of light. Let your children make halos out of gold rope from the Christmas tree. Ask them to think of ways in which they acted like a messenger today. Remind them of their good deeds, such as 1) They answered the phone and gave you the message. 2) They told you the dog needed water or the baby needed a bottle. Therefore, say they may wear a halo since they acted like a loving messenger (angel) today. Tell about your belief in angels and how angels help you.

WEDNESDAY: * Show **symbols for north, east, south and west** on a map. Then put Mary and Joseph in the northern part of your room. Label it "Nazareth". Put the shepherds in the south by a sign labeled "Hills of Judah." Put the Wise Men in the east. Words on the signs will help your children to become more self sufficient in reading. Hide Jesus until Christmas morning.

THURSDAY: Children learn best by being actively involved in the learning process. Help your daughter pretend to be Mary. Put a cloth around her head and shoulders. Tell her good things about Mary. Let your son wear a halo and pretend to be Gabriel while you summarize Luke 1:29-38. A seven year old can start to read parts from Luke alone, let your child try using a Child's **Bible** which is easier to read. A **Bible** is God's word.

FRIDAY * Tell your children, people use **lights** as a symbol meaning Jesus, the light of the world, is coming. This would be a good time to decorate outside the house with lights. Inform your children the Bible says, "God is **light** " and Jesus said, "I am the light of the world." Jesus came into the world to "bring us light". Jesus is the light which helps us see things more clearly.

SATURDAY : * **Bells** are symbols of ringing in the Good News of Jesus' birth. Gather bells you have in the house. Explain how in the old days, people didn't have newspapers, T.V. or radios so the church bells would ring when people were born or died. People would rush to the church to find out the news. On Christmas Day many churches will be ringing bells to tell of Christ's birth. Your children will enjoy singing their favorite songs and ringing the bells.

## SECOND WEEK IN ADVENT

SUNDAY: * Light two candles. This week, the second candle will be **a symbol for Joseph** since his part is important in the story. The angel will come to Joseph in a dream. Some angels come to people (like Mary ) while they are awake. Some angels deliver messages while people are asleep (like Joseph). Read Matthew 1:18-21, explain **dreams** can be symbols. Ask what the worst part and the most enjoyable part was of a special dream they had. Then have them draw pictures of the dream to help them have control of their feelings.

MONDAY: * Read Luke 2:1-3. Explain a census is a form of counting. Let your children make a census taker for their set or play the **census chart** game. Have one child roll the dice. Then he may add the dice together and use the larger number or choose to use the number on each die separately. Let him draw the item(s) for the number(s) he threw. Twelve is wild, he may draw whatever number he needs. Then it's your turn. The winner is the one which gets all the items drawn first on his paper.

1= One person ( Jesus, Mary or Joseph )

2- Two angels

3= Three Wise Men

4= Four candles

5= Five stars

6- Six wreaths

7- Seven trees

8- Eight lights

9= Nine halos

10- Ten candy canes

11- Eleven bells

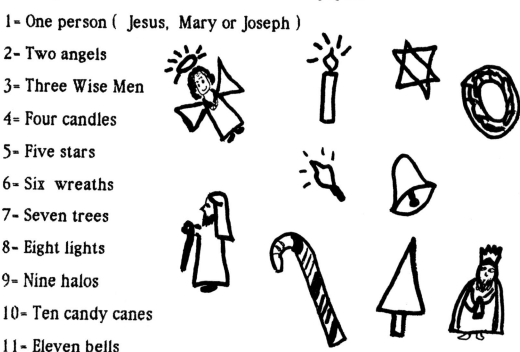

TUESDAY: * Read Luke 2: 4. Review why Mary and Joseph had to travel to Bethlehem. In the family room **tables** can be symbols for different towns. Give each table a name of a town that Mary and Joseph will travel thru. Have children make townspeople or town signs. Look at a map in your bible. Follow the route going through Nain, Sychar in upper Samaria, Jacob's well in lower Samaria, Jerusalem and to Bethlehem. Move Holy family to first town.

WEDNESDAY: * **Christmas trees are symbols** of many things. Martin Luther brought one inside and put candles on it because it reminded him of the stars shining through the trees. Others feel since God made trees they are symbols of the things God has made for us. They remind us of Jesus' family tree and how we are part of God's family. The top point of trees reminds us to look up to God. Move Mary and Joseph to upper Samaria. Add trees to the area. They can be made from pine cones.

THURSDAY: * Explain Jesus and his father were both **carpenters.** Ask what a carpenter does? Some will guess, "He takes care of carpets." To learn about their job let the children work like a carpenter, using a hammer and nails.

FRIDAY: * Have your children make a sign for a carpenter shop using pictures of tools as symbols. Place it in Nazareth near Joseph's home. Name things Joseph may have used. Cut out pictures of tools from newspaper ads. For an opportunity to practice large muscle skills teach them to use a saw to make a manger to hold hay and later to hold Jesus.

SATURDAY: Move Mary and Joseph to Jacob's well in lower Samaria.

Let your children put Mary on the donkey and ride her from town to town. Put animals in the stable. Although **animals** are not mentioned in the story, a prophecy from Isaiah 1:3 inspired people to believe an ox and a donkey were at Jesus' birth. Isaiah 1: 3 says, "The ox knows its owner, and the ass it's master's crib, but Israel does not know." Therefore, this famous prophecy inspired people to believe these two animals were present and understood the spiritual truths which the Jewish leaders did not. The donkey is thought to have carried Mary to Bethlehem and Egypt.

## THIRD WEEK IN ADVENT

SUNDAY: * Light three candles. The third candle can be called the Shepherd's candle. Jesus is called the Good **Shepherd** because He watches over us. The shepherds which came to see Jesus in the stable represented uneducated and poor people but ones with faith enough to follow the angels' directions. Move Mary and Joseph to the fourth town, Jerusalem. A valuable experience is to let your child dictate part of the Christmas story to you. After you have written it down help your child with the concept of reading. A child can usually read a story which he has dictated.

MONDAY: * Make lots of **lambs** and shepherds. If you bought a set, your children can still make some from the pattern to add to your set. Children don't mind mixing their figures with ones you bought. Explain people are called God's lambs. Sometimes we get lost. Attention span should be getting longer. Have them retell the story to show how much of it they remember,

TUESDAY: *Review why we have **candy canes.** They look like a shepherd's staff. Upside down the candy cane makes the "J" for Jesus. Inform your children if they can help someone today, they will get a candy cane.

31

WEDNESDAY: * Let a child put Mary on the donkey and take her through each town on the route. Put a smiley face on every sign that can be read. Start in Nazareth like Joseph and Mary did. **Nazareth** means branch. It reminds us Jesus was from the branch of Jesse and David.

THURSDAY: Children can add a piece of straw to the manger for each good deed they do. This will make Jesus' bed soft. Another year have them write the good **deed** on a strip of paper to represent straw and place it in the manger. The visual child comprehends by seeing. Let him see you write the good deed. He is becoming aware of words. The audio child gains knowledge by hearing the deed read. Let the kinesthetic child place it in the manger.

FRIDAY *Tell how one angel came to the shepherds. The angel told them Jesus would be wrapped in **swaddling cloths**. Then many angels appeared and there was a bright light and the shepherds were afraid. Let your children express feelings about when they were afraid. Let your children make swaddling strips out of an old linen towel for a doll. Explain the baby was wrapped snugly to make his bones straight.

SATURDAY: Since children enjoy discussions, talk about Carols. Learn "Away in the Manger." Ask what a **manger** is and why it was in the stable.

## FOURTH WEEK IN ADVENT
SUNDAY: * Light all four candles. Show how many days remain until Christmas. Eve. Mention when they will be going to church and why it will be special. Remind them they will be able to open their presents when Jesus is in the manger.

Pass out a fourth figure. Since every year there will be a different number of days left in the fourth week, discuss as many of the symbols as you have time to do until Christmas Eve.

## ACTIVITIES FOR SIX DAYS OR LESS:

1 **Star:** The Wise Men were watching for a special star to tell them when Jesus would be born. To help develop their language skills have the children explain why some people put a star on their tree. Make paper or cookie stars.

2 **Gold:** Wise Men brought gold to Jesus. Gold was a gift to give a King. Jesus was King of Kings. Cut gold off a Christmas card and give it to Jesus.

3 **Frankincense:** Priests in Mary's day burned frankincense in the temples. It was a gift to give a High Priest. Jesus is our High Priest. Burn some incense.

4. **Myrrh:** Baby oil feels like myrrh. Put it on their hands. Explain myrrh was put on people's bodies after they died. Then they were wrapped in cloth.

5. **Poinsettia:** The flower looks like the star the wise men followed. Look for one in a flower shop or on a card.

6. **Inn:** Similar to motels of today. Now a symbol for homes too crowded to have room for Jesus. Name symbols in your house that honor Jesus.

**CHRISTMAS EVE** To build a family tradition, repeat the things you did in Chapter One for Christmas Eve and Day. At this age, children often have a desire to pray. Make this a special project as they journey to Bethlehem.

**TWELVE DAYS OF CHRISTMAS ACTIVITIES:**

1. **CHRISTMAS DAY**: Move angels to shepherds to tell them about Jesus.

2. Move shepherds to manger. Compare your child's birth to Jesus'.

3. Move shepherds back to hillside. Enjoy dramatic play with costumes.

4. Explain a Creche has figures of Joseph, Mary, infant, shepherds and Magi.

5. The Bible doesn't say how many Wise Men there were. Your children can develop small eye-hand coordination, by making many Wise Men for the set.

6. Let the children create skits as they move the Wise Men south.

7. Move Wise Men closer to Bethlehem.  Read Matthew 2:1-12

8. New Year's day is the eighth day.  All Jewish babies in Mary's day got their name on the eighth day, as did Jesus, according to the custom.  Ask the children if they can connect personal experiences caused by their name.

9. Let the children write thank you notes or draw pictures of all their gifts.

10. Move the Wise Men closer. Have children dictate a Christmas story to you.

11. Matthew 2:11 tells, when the Wise Men came, they entered the house. Put Mary, Joseph and Jesus in a house. Make a crib out of a little box.

12. Make symbols to represent the three gifts from the Wise Men. This is called the Twelfth Day of Christmas. On the evening of the Twelfth Day is the start of Epiphany.

EPIPHANY: This is the day the Wise Men arrive. Some people wait until the sixth of January to exchange gifts. This is the beginning of spreading the word of Jesus beyond the Jewish people. Decide what four new figures your child would like next year. Try to buy them on sale this week.

ACTIVITY: Having many reminders of Jesus in your home helps keep Christ in **Christ**mas. Many people need to gain the knowledge of ways to see the Christ Child in the materialism and confusion of the holiday. Teaching the meanings of the Christian symbols can be fun and give spiritual significance to otherwise insignificant decorations.

Here is a game called, "**Make Room for Jesus**". Play it with your children
1. Give each child a sheet of paper and a pencil.
2. Read a word from the list of the symbols below.
3. If a child can give the meaning of the word, the child can draw one line or a circle. Let the second child do the same.
4. Four lines makes a room. Two more lines makes a roof. Three more lines make a bed and one circle and a few lines makes Jesus.

5. Continue until someone wins. First person who draws Jesus in a bed in the house wins. For help, use the glossary or review this chapter.

1. Advent Wreath
2. Angels
3. Bells
4. Birthday Cake
5. Candles
6. Candy
7. Carols
8. Christmas Tree
9. Creche
10. Doves
11. Epiphany ( Twelfth Night)
12. Frankincense
13. Gifts
14. Gold
15. Holly and Ivy
16. Horns
17. Myrrh
18. Poinsettia
19. Star
20. Swaddling Clothes
21. Wreath

Missed a couple meanings. Substitute these for the ones you didn't get
22. Lights
23. Hanukkah or Xmas
24 . Manger
25. Wise Men

Next year make up your own words and build more rooms. Then check if every room in your real home has at least one symbol to remind you of dear Jesus. Put a wreath on your door. An Advent wreath on the dining room table. A Creche in the living room. A candy cane on your bedroom door. Place doves in the bathroom and swaddling clothes on the dolls. Then you have won the game of "Making Room For Jesus In Your Home". Now be sure you have made room for Jesus in your heart. Accepting Jesus in your heart wins you eternal life. That's the best gift of all at Christmas.

# CHAPTER 3

## OUT OF THE MOUTHS OF BABES

### Third Through Seventh graders grow with a Christian Vocabulary.

Words are the keys to thoughts and ideas, and some children haven't been given the keys to unlock the meanings of many words. Their versions are unintentional confusion. A few examples of misquoted stories from children: 1. God's name is Harold, as in "Our Father who is in heaven, 'Harold' be thy name." 2. The Holy Family made the flight into Egypt with Pontius, 'the Pilot' flying the plane. 3. Joseph took an insect with him because the angel told Joseph to take Mary and 'flea' to Egypt. 4. The children thought the swaddling cloth must be a blanket with holes since they heard when Jesus was born, he was wrapped in swaddling cloth and the 'Holy' Comforter was with Him. 5. The Wise Men were firemen because they came from 'afar' (a fire). 6. The shepherds out in the field "washed" their sheep by night. 7. The Epistles were the wives of the Apostles. 8. Joshua led the Hebrews in the battle of "Geritol". 9. Lot's wife was a pillar of salt by day and a ball of fire by night. 10. A child reciting the rosary said, "Hail Mary full of grapes," and repeating the Seventh Commandment as " Thou shalt not admit adultery." 11. Mary and Joseph joined a " Dodge" caravan on the road.

Your responsibility this Advent requires you to build a word path your children can follow to know Jesus. This year the children will not be given direction on how to move the figures. They learned how in Chapters One and can now produce their own productions. They should enjoy reading, listening to the story and repeating it. They should gather facts and compare stories.

To build a strong foundation it is preferable to utilized the information in the previous chapters.

If you have just purchased this book, you should initially expose your children to the simple routine in Chapter One and the concrete symbols in Chapter Two. The earlier chapters can generate enough interest for this age. However, fifth graders might desire to create a more challenging Nativity set. The story becomes more significant if the children contribute something in the way of a set which gives them room for discovering their talents.

When children of this age group hear Joseph was a **carpenter**, they often think he took care of carpets. Therefore, an experience can add to word power. The family can make a wooden set together. Children can feel the roughness of the wood before it is sanded and the smoothness afterwards. As they put the patterns on the wood, their mind can wander to a time when Jesus and his father worked together. As an adult helps them cut out the figures on a jig saw they can smell the saw dust. They can use their imagination in painting the historical figures. The important part is to have the figures available when needed for the story even if you have to buy a small set. A new figure should be added each week. Chapter One's patterns serviceable.

When the Bethlehem Lutheran Girl Scouts visited our home each girl was given a different silhouette figure made of felt. As the children told the story they put the figures on a larger piece of felt. The leader said at their next Scout meeting they had fun copying and trading until each girl had a set.

## FIRST WEEK IN ADVENT

SUNDAY: Light the first candle on the Advent Wreath. Review **Advent** means coming. Tell your children the Jewish people waited for hundreds of years for the coming of the **Messiah ( means anointed).** Leaders were anointed with oil. Christmas is the celebration of the coming of Jesus who was the awaited Messiah. Lay the foundation of the Christmas story by reading the often forgotten part Luke 1: 7. Let the children set up their nativity set and review the facts they remember. An ongoing project for building a Christian vocabulary is to learn a new word every day. On your refrigerator post a permanent sentence such as: "The word for today is _____. ." Every day post a new word and talk about it. Then both you and your children should use it throughout the day. A project like this can create an impetus of its own which will encourage exploration of new words.

39

MONDAY: Read Luke1:8-9. Zachariah is in the **temple.** Point out that a temple was similar to a church. The priest was the only one allowed inside the holy inner part which was behind a **veil** (heavy curtain).

TUESDAY: Read Luke1:10. People believed their prayers rose up quicker to heaven in the smoke of good **incense.** Burn and smell some incense.

WEDNESDAY: Read Luke1:11-17. An angel appeared and told Zachariah his son, (John) would be a **prophet.** A prophet is someone who foretells what is going to happen. A **prophecy** is what he tells. In the Old **Testament** in Isaiah 40: 3-5 and Mal.3:1, it was told a prophet like Elijah would come before the Messiah. The angel said this prophecy would be fulfilled through John. This is the first prophecy in the Christmas story ( See Chapter Nine ).

THURSDAY: A **testament** is a division of the Bible. Point out the Bible has an old and a new **testament.** Explain the Old Testament was written before Jesus was born. The New one is about His birth and His life. Read Luke1:18 to 20 and explain Zachariah had prayed for a long time to have a child. Yet he was surprised when the angel told him God was going to answer his prayers.

FRIDAY: * Read to Luke 1:17- 20. Explain what it means to be **mute.** Do not use the word dumb. People who can not talk are not dumb. It's a misleading word. This is a great age to learn **sign language.** Use books from a library to learn signing. Some excellent sources are: Sign Language Fun by Sesame Street by Linda Bove; How to Speak With Your Hands by Elaine Costello; Talk to the Deaf and The Joy of Signing by Lottie Riekehof.

SATURDAY: * Read Luke 1: 21-25. First graders can learn to **sign** "Away in the Manger" and second graders can learn to sign "Silent Night".

### Part of "Away in a Manager" in Sign Language

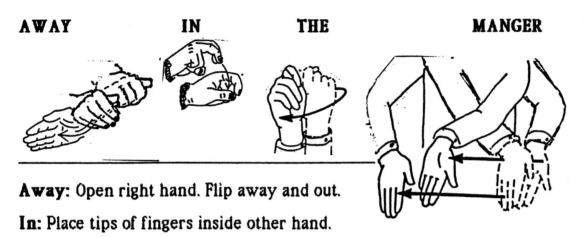

AWAY       IN       THE       MANGER

**Away:** Open right hand. Flip away and out.

**In:** Place tips of fingers inside other hand.

**The:** Make the letter T with right hand. Palm in and then twist out.

**Manger:** Open B both hands fingers down, left palm out, right palm in. Hold at left side of body then slide to right.

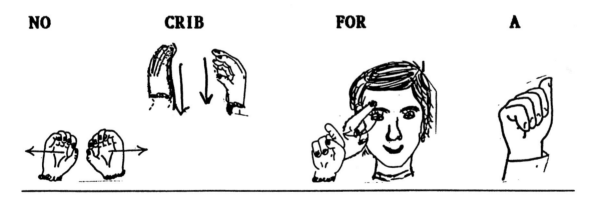

NO       CRIB       FOR       A

**No:** Place the "O" hands in front of you, palms facing out; bring both hands to the sides, still in the "O" position. The two zeros indicate none.

**Crib:** Make the number four shape with both hands. Lower slightly.

**For:** Make number one shape RH palm in. Place finger tip on forehead, twist wrist and point finger tip forward.

**A:** Make letter " a ".

**BED          LITTLE          LORD          JESUS**

Bed : Put right palm on right cheek and tilt head to right.

Little: Fingers out. Move close together.

Lord: Make "L" shape with hand. Move from collar to other side

and lower part of body.

Jesus: Make an open "B" with both hands, palms facing out.  Place tip of right

middle finger on left palm. Then place left middle finger on right palm.


## SECOND WEEK IN ADVENT

SUNDAY: Light two candles.  Read Luke 1:26-27. Place an angel by Mary.

Explain **betrothal** means an engagement.


MONDAY: Luke1:27 tells Joseph is a descendant of King David.  **Descendant**

means forefather or relative from the past.


TUESDAY:  Read Luke 1: 27-35.  Two prophecies are mentioned here about

Mary.  In Gen. 3:15, it tells the Messiah would be born of a women.  In Isaiah

7:14, the prophecy says the Messiah would be born of a virgin.  Since children

often sing about **virgin** Mary, it's a good time to explain this term such as a

woman who has not been married and has not had any babies.

WEDNESDAY: Read Luke 1:36-56. Explain **kinswoman** means relative. Make a figure of Elizabeth, place her by Mary for three days to help remember Mary visited there for three months.

THURSDAY: Read Luke 1: 57-66. Review **sign** language lesson and make signs to Zachariah. Read Luke 1: 67-69. Zachariah says, " blessed be the Lord God, who has raised up a **Horn of Salvation**". The message carrier is the horn carrying the news our Salvation is coming. Decorate the house with horns.

FRIDAY: Read Luke1: 70-79. John was to come before the Messiah. A prophecy said the Messiah would have a **forerunner**. This was a person who ran before a King and yelled "the King is coming" or a person who went before to make the road smooth. John's job would be to let people know Jesus was coming. Review word and sign list. Words change and grow. Children haven't lived long enough to always have full understanding of many common words.

SATURDAY: Vocabulary accounts for approximately 60% of comprehension. To build word knowledge, the key words are **exposure** and **usage**. Retrieve the vocabulary list from where it is posted. It should have ten words on it. On a strip of paper, write each new word your child can read and use in a sentence and place it in the manger. In Chapter 2, the children put a piece of straw in the manger for every good deed. Both deeds and words can make Jesus' manger soft for him. Help your children to **research** other Christian words, their origin and histories.

## THIRD WEEK IN ADVENT

SUNDAY: Light the third candle. Read Matthew 1:18-25, Mary is **conceived** by the Holy Spirit. Ask what your child has learned in his sex education class.

MONDAY: Read Luke 2:1. Explain what a **census** is. Introduce the names of Caesar Augustus ( means Kingly ) and Quirinius. Children at this age are usually interested in historical stories and famous people of the past.

TUESDAY: Read Luke 2:2-4. Review the **geography** of the Christmas story. Nazareth was in the north. Bethlehem was in the south. The shepherds were in the hills near Jerusalem. Studying maps enriches stories of Jesus' later life.

Courtesy of Grand Rapids Press -photograph by John R. Fulton Jr.1979

WEDNESDAY: Discuss the **route** the Holy Family may have taken. Study a map to decide if your children want them to go by the "Way of the Sea" going west from Nazareth to Caesarea and then south to Joppa and to Jerusalem or to go through **Nain.** Use **sequence** skills while planning route.

THURSDAY: Characteristics of children of this age are honesty, fairness and a sense of guilt. Their conscience is an integral part of them at this age. They have begun to differentiate between **fantasy** and **faith.** Discuss what it means to live like a Christian and to know the real Christmas story. Have them pick Christmas cards and postage stamps which honor Jesus.

FRIDAY: Move Mary and Joseph closer each day to the stable in Bethlehem. **Bethlehem** means house of bread. Discuss why Jesus is the "bread of life". Children enjoy how and why questions. Study the "B" glossary words.

SATURDAY: Planned rather than accidental teaching is best. Knowing the meaning of words will increase the knowledge of the **main idea** of the Christmas story. Challenge children to memorize the Christmas story a little each day so they may tell it as their 'Christmas gift' to the family.

**FOURTH WEEK IN ADVENT**

SUNDAY: Light the four candles. Review words introduced in earlier chapters: **stable, manger, inn and halos.** Put stars on every word they know on their chart. This age needs and responds to praise. They are sensitive to criticism. For this age, use timelines and chronological stories. Christmas can be one to seven days from now, pick one of these project for each day left:

1. Move the Wise Men closer to Jerusalem.  Explain the term **Magi** means astrologer, one who studied the stars.  This is why they were thought wise. This is the time to get books about **constellations** from the Library.

2. Discuss words in the **Glossary** from **Abiding** through **Ark**.  Many children only know about Noah's Ark and some think his wife was Joan of **Ark**. Most have never heard of the **Ark** which was kept in the temple in Jerusalem. Jesus was carried to this temple as a baby.

3. Give a candy cane to all your children who can read the "c" **words in the glossary** and know the meaning of the words (especially candy cane ).

4. Tell how King Herod had scribes working for him.  **Scribes** were men who copied and studied the Old Testament.  They held that position because they could read and write which many people could not do in those days.

5. Read Luke 2:6-7.  Explain why Jesus was wrapped in **swaddling** cloth. Some ethnic groups still wrap babies this way to make the bones strong and back straight.  Use the **cause and effect** skill here.  Some say the cloth was a symbol of the linen Jesus would be wrapped in after his death.

6. Move Mary and Joseph to the inn and later on Xmas Eve to the stable.

CHRISTMAS EVE: Read the "Night Before Christ Birth" found in Chapter 11.

CHRISTMAS DAY : Sing " Happy Birthday Dear Jesus" and make him a Birthday cake. Learn a new word from the glossary, each day during the next 12 days.

**EPIPHANY**: . Hope you had fun learning the meaning of words along with your children. May the Christmas Story always be exciting and not **monotonous**. A child thought monotonous meant a husband could only have one wife. May Christmas be a marriage of joy, honor and love for Jesus.

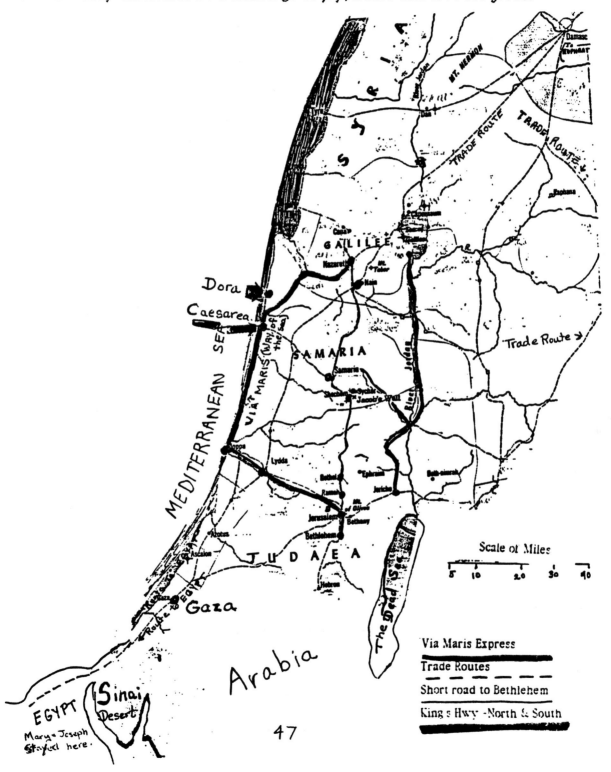

47

# CHAPTER 4

## JESUS' MOTHER, MARY THE TEENAGER

### Teens discover how Old Testament relates to Christmas Story

Many feel Mary was just a teenager when the angel came to her with the news she would have a baby and call Him Jesus. How would a teenage Mary today respond to such news? Would she abort the baby? When the Junior High group from Asbury United Methodist Church came to our home for a tour, we were impressed with their manners and intelligence. Like many teens, they were intrigued with the Holy Family's Jewish background and the Old Testament prophecies. We hope they left with an understanding of the fundamentals of Judaism. We need to emphasize the similarities between the heritage of our Jewish roots and our present practices. We need to show how much we share instead of what divides us. We need to show how the New Testament is a fulfillment of the Old. This chapter gives the background of some Jewish customs, words and important names.

Your teens will soon be starting their own traditions in their own homes. Use this chapter to learn from each other. May this chapter guide your teens to be role model parents of the future.

First, arrange the Nativity set in the areas for the Christmas story, as in Chapter One. Each chapter builds on the preceding one. Therefore, be sure to be familiar with the information in the previous chapters and incorporate those ideas. This year added emphasis will be on information about Jewish customs. Continue to give each teen a new figure each Sunday in Advent.

If your family hasn't been giving a new figure to each child on each Sunday, why not at this time buy a collectible which your teen could take possession of when s/he marries.

An unbreakable pewter collection cost about one hundred dollars or $16 a piece. A Precious Moment set cost about $25 for each piece. Both of these sets have a limited number of figures. Fontinine sets have an unending number of figures for about $25 each. If your teenagers prefer to make their own set, get a Library book explaining how to make a paper mache set.

## FIRST WEEK IN ADVENT

SUNDAY: Light one candle of the Advent Wreath. Each day there will be an important word in **bold** printing. Start with the reading of Luke 1: 5-9. The Lord's sanctuary was in the **temple**. The first **temple** had been started in 20 B.C. and was still not completed forty-six years later. The temple was sacred because an angel had shown David where to build it. The first temple was proposed by David but built by his son, Solomon. This temple was burned by the Babylonians when they captured Jerusalem. Then the Jews began the second temple in 537 B.C. The **Holy of Holies** was then empty as the **Ark of the Covenant** had disappeared. Then Herod tore down the second temple to build the third. This was his project and a monument to him. Jesus soon after he is born will be brought to this temple as was the custom.

MONDAY: Read Luke 1:9-11. Explain the people gathered outside while the incense burned since they felt their prayers lifted to God in the fine smoke. **Frankincense** was the finest incense and a fitting gift to give a High Priest.

TUESDAY: The last utterance of the Old Testament (Malachi 4: 5-6 ) stated Elijah would reappear as the **Messiah's harbinger**. The angel in Luke 1:11

tells Zachariah his child would be the one to whom the prophecy pointed. John will have the spirit and power of Elijah. He will go before the Lord and prepare the way for him. This is the first prophecy fulfilled in the Christmas story. Read Luke 1:12-25. Zachariah first expressed fear and Gabriel said to him, "Do not be afraid, for your prayers have been heard." How would your teens feel if they saw an angel? In Luke 1: 19, Zach expresses doubt. The angel was perturbed and silenced him until after John's birth.

WEDNESDAY: Luke 1: 26-31 This is called the **Annunciation**. This fulfills two prophecies: 1. The Messiah would be born of a woman. 2. He'd be born of a virgin. Explain the male part of the conception of Jesus was taken over by the Holy spirit of God. No one else in human history has been conceived that way. **Jesus was born of a virgin.**

THURSDAY: Read Luke 1: 32-35. It fulfills the prophecy the Messiah would be of the **line of David.** Isa.9:6-7 says he will be heir to the throne of David.

FRIDAY: Luke 1:36-45, tells about Elizabeth and Mary's visit to her. Luke 46 to 55 is called the **Magnificat** or the Song of Mary. This song is similar to Hannah's song of praise in 1 Samuel 2:1-10. Mary used words from scripture which were familiar to her. Read the directions and make a Jesse Tree. Then add a tag with Mary's name to a branch.

**Information for the Jesse Tree :** Isaiah 11:1 tells us: " There shall come forth a shoot from the stump of Jesse, and a branch shall grow out of his roots." Isaiah 53: 2 says " Like a sapling he grew up before him. like a root in arid ground." The Old Testament was written to relate the anticipation of the

50

coming of Christ through the line of Jesse. The Messianic Strain blends the many Old Testament diverse books into one. Isa. 9:6-7 says the Messiah will be heir to the throne of David. Matthew 1:5-8 tells us Jesse fathered David. King David fathered Solomon with Bathsheba as the mother. Solomon's line goes down to Jacob who fathered Joseph. When Joseph's wife Mary had Jesus, the prophecy was fulfilled, that the Messiah would be of the house of David. Luke 3:23 tells Jesse fathered David and David fathered Nathan as well as other sons. Nathan's line fathered Heli, who fathered Mary, who gave birth to Jesus, our Lord.

**Directions for making a Jesse Tree**: Put a branch from a tree in a bottle. Then make paper ornaments with names and designs on them. For Jesus draw a manger and print "Jesus". Hang it on the top of the branch. For Joseph, make a hammer, for David a crown and for Jacob a ladder. Another way to portray the Jesse Tree is to get a piece of driftwood. Place a reclining figure at the bottom to be Jesse. Then place little figures going to the top where Mary is holding Jesus. Talk about your family tree and show your teens their family tree in their baby book. Make ornaments depicting your family to put on the tree.

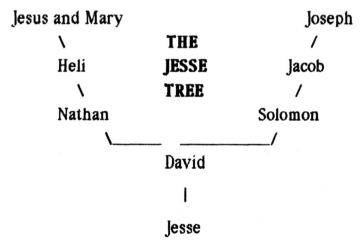

```
Jesus and Mary                        Joseph
        \           THE                 /
      Heli         JESSE              Jacob
        \           TREE               /
    Nathan                          Solomon
            \_____      _____/
                    David
                      |
                    Jesse
```

Put these ornaments on your Xmas tree, if you don't have a Jesse Tree.

SATURDAY: Read Luke 1: 56-66. John was **circumcised** and received his name and when he was eight days old. It was the male's first rite into the covenant of his people. It consists of removing the foreskin of the penis. The new covenant of baptism replaces the ceremony of circumcision. John was born to a **barren** women past child-bearing age.


**SECOND WEEK IN ADVENT**

SUNDAY: Light two candles. Read Luke 1: 67-80. **Zachariah's prophecy** about his son, John, is called the **Benedictus.** He tells his son will prepare the way of the Messiah. Benedictus is Latin for blessed, which is the first word of his praise to God in verse 68 of Luke Chapter one. He praises God for the act of salvation that is about to come and emphasizes John will be the forerunner of the Messiah. It is used as liturgy in some churches.


MONDAY: Change to the Gospel of Matthew. Read Chapter 1:1 which says Christ was a descendant of King David and Abraham. This fulfills the prophecy of Gen. 12: 3 that through **Abraham** all families of the earth would be blessed. Matt.1: 2-16, fulfills Num. 24:17, there shall come a star out of Jacob. Jesus is the star from the line of Jacob. Matthew wrote a global gospel with a Jewish accent. When you read Jesus' family tree, you will see it has embarrassing individuals. His **genealogy also** goes beyond Jews to include several ethnic groups from the Middle East during Israel's history. Jesus never denied His ancestry. Christmas is a time to learn to accept people regardless of culture, gender, race and reputation and avoid demeaning anyone else's heritage. Jesus came for all. Jesus came in human form, The Son of man, and more importantly, He was the long expected Messiah. The word became flesh and dwelled among us. Start to move the Holy Family to Bethlehem. Read Luke 2.

TUESDAY: Read Matthew 1:3. Teen-age girls are interested in the women of the **genealogy** who were touched by scandal and called foreigners & sinners. They served God's purpose and became better persons. **Tamar's** story found in Gen. 38: 1-30 tells she was widowed by the first born of Judah. She then married the second born. He refused to consummate the marriage before he died, leaving her childless and without support. Her father-in-law avoided the responsibility to provide her with another husband and sent her back to her home village. Tamar resorted to trickery, acting as a prostitute, she caused Judah to father **an heir.** Judah, when exposed as the father, explained, " She (Tamar) is more righteous than I" (Genesis 38: 26). He then provided her with economic security. The child continued the line which eventually led to Jesus.

WEDNESDAY: Read Matthew 1:5. **Rahab** is found in Josh 2: 1-24 and 6: 22-25. She was a harlot who protected two Hebrew spies in Jericho in exchange for her own family's protection from the Israelites who surrounded the city. She is praised in Hebrew 11: 31 for her faith and in James 2: 25 for faithful action. She later married a Hebrew and **gave birth to Boaz** in Bethlehem. He was **David's** great-grandfather. Add a tag with David's name to the Jesse Tree.

THURSDAY: Reread Matthew 1:5. Inform your teens, the **Ruth** in Jesus' genealogy, is a Moab from the nation which began after the fall of Sodom when Lot committed incest with his daughters (Gen. 19: 30-38). The Moabites became bitter enemies of Israel. Ruth's Jewish husband died and left her without sons. She went with her mother-in-law, Naomi, to Israel and married Boaz. A tradition says when Boaz took Ruth to be his bride they started their family in the same room in which 1100 years later Christ would be born.

Ruth became the mother of **Obed**, making her David's great-grandmother. The Song of Ruth, "where thou goest I will go," from Ruth 1:1 is often played at weddings.

FRIDAY: Read Matthew 1: 5-6. The ancestors of Christ were racially mixed with Gentiles and Hebrew because of Ruth. Obed fathered **Jesse** who fathered King **David.** The coming "Branch" reviving out of the stump of Jesse, who is mentioned in Isaiah 11:1 & 53:2, is Jesus. It is interesting that Jesus' mother came from **Nazareth which** also means **"Branch."** Add Jesse to Jesse Tree.

SATURDAY: Read Matthew 1:6-7. **David** was the father of Solomon. David's wife was the ex-wife of Uriah, the Hittite. She is unnamed by Matthew but she is **Bathsheba.** In 2 Samuel 11:1 through 12: 25, she attracts King David while she is bathing in ritual obedience, cleaning herself from her monthly flow. David commits adultery with Bathsheba who becomes pregnant. David causes her husband, Uriah, to be murdered. She loses the child fathered by David. They marry and she gives birth to **Solomon.** His line leads to Joseph, husband of Mary. David later fathers **Nathan,** whose line leads to Mary. Add Solomon and Nathan names to Jesse Tree. Put Jesse by the stump with David above Jesse. Put Nathan on the branch above David's right. Mary is above Nathan. Solomon is above David on his left. Put Joseph's tag above Solomon.

## THIRD WEEK IN ADVENT

SUNDAY: Add a new figure to your set. Light the third candle. Some people use a pink candle for the third week. Have **a Mystery Dinner** to observe this joyful day. Look over the menu and try guessing the foods. Then let your teens invite friends over and help your teens serve this dinner menu.

**Mystery Dinner preparations:**

1. Invite six people to an Advent Mystery dinner.

2. Select at least three people to serve your guests.

3. Close off your kitchen so the guests can not see the food (it's a mystery).

4. Place condiments, like cocktail sauce, mustard, mayo, catsup, salt and pepper on the table (clues to ordering) but not silverware, dishes or cups.

5. Set up your kitchen with items grouped together for the convenience of your servers.

**Suggestion for easy grouping of items:**

1. Place on counter: Silverware: spoon = dipper;  fork = found in road;  Knife = Herod's dagger;  nap-kin = sleeping relative

2. Food on counter: pickles = Kosher food; Bread = Bethlehem; Angel food cake = Angel's Delight; candy cane = Shepherd's staff;

3. Keep hot food on stove: Angel Hair noodles = Gabriel's hair; ; Potatoes = Mary "eyes" Joseph; a Wise Man's gift = Gold(en) corn

4. Place in ice chest: Main food: Ham = Not kosher; 3 shrimp = Wee 3 Kings; Deviled eggs = Herod's food; Caesar salad = Caesar Augustus' fame;

5. Keep in refrigerator: Drinks: water = Jacob's well; Pop = Joseph's role; Tea = Last letter of Christ; Desserts: Doves ice cream mini pieces = 2nd x-mas gift

**Guests arrive:**

1. Welcome friends to Bethlehem. Tell them to sit on the chair by their name tag which is in code. They will have to figure out their "mystery" name. Bill's code name could be "money" or "part of a duck". David means "Beloved" so that could be his code name. A teacher could be "Wise Man. Someone stubborn could be "donkey". A motel owner could be "an innkeeper. Try to use names which relate to Jesus' birth.  Give each person a Mystery menu.

## MYSTERY DINNER MENU

| | 1 | 2 | 3 | 4 | 5 | 6 | 7 |
|---|---|---|---|---|---|---|---|
| Joseph's Role | | | | | | | |
| Mary eyes Joseph | | | | | | | |
| Wise Men's Gift | | | | | | | |
| Star shaped dipper | | | | | | | |
| Partridge's home | | | | | | | |
| 2nd X-mas gift | | | | | | | |
| Sleeping relative | | | | | | | |
| Wee 3 Kings | | | | | | | |
| Angel's delight | | | | | | | |
| Herod's dagger | | | | | | | |
| Herod's food | | | | | | | |
| Found in road | | | | | | | |
| In Jacob's well | | | | | | | |
| Shepherd's staff | | | | | | | |
| Augustus' fame | | | | | | | |
| Last letter of Christ | | | | | | | |
| Stable food | | | | | | | |
| Top of Gabriel | | | | | | | |
| Not Kosher | | | | | | | |
| Kosher food | | | | | | | |
| " Go to" Egypt | | | | | | | |
| Bethlehem | | | | | | | |

2. Give everyone a pen and have them write their code name on their menu.

3. Instruct friends on how to order from the menu. For their first course, they need to pick three items they want. Then they have to put an X in the first column after those items. They can not pick more or less than three items.

4. Explain the menu is from a Bethlehem Inn. Therefore, the language must be decoded. For example: If it says, " a cow that has just had a baby calf," they would be ordering something that is **decaffe**inated (like coffee).

A snow pile might be a pile of white potatoes or a dish of white ice cream.

5. A waiter will pick up their order. The waiter will go to the kitchen and get the paper plate with their code name on it so the menu and plate will always match. He returns with just the three items they ordered. If they ordered ice cream, green beans and olives, they will have to use their fingers since they didn't order their silverware. The waiter then makes your X's into stars.

6. After they have eaten what they ordered in the first column, they may mark 3 x's in the next column. They do this seven times.

7. After they have had their seven-course meal, they may enter the kitchen and serve themselves a second helping of anything they really liked.

8. At the end of the party explain what each item meant.


MONDAY: Read Matthew 1:15-25. It tells us that **Jacob** was the father of Joseph. It also fulfills the prophecy that the Messiah would be born of a virgin. " The virgin is with child whom they will call Immanuel." This name means **"God-is-in-us"** and "God with us". Jesus came and lived among his people. He walked with the problems of the day. Jesus can help your teens and give them the power to do the job they need to do. The name Jesus means "Jehovah is salvation." Jesus is called by both names. The word became flesh and dwelled among us. Put Jacob's tag above Solomon on Tree.

TUESDAY : Turn back to Luke and read 2: 1-3.  God used the ungodly **to fulfill His prophecy in Micah 5:2** which says the Messiah would be born in Bethlehem.  Caesar Augustus caused Mary and Joseph, from Nazareth, to travel to Bethlehem when it was time for Mary to give birth.  The census was taken by the registration of people according to their tribe, family and house.  In the first chapter of Numbers this was very common.

WEDNESDAY: In Matthew the lineage of Joseph was traced to help us see his importance as a foster father.  Read Luke 2:4-6.  It reiterates the Messiah had to be born of the line of Abraham (Gen..12 :3-7; Gen. 17: ).  He had to be from the tribe of Judah (Ps. 72: 10;  Is a. 60: 3, 6, 9).  He had to be from the house of David. ( 2 Sam. 7:12).  Joseph fulfilled these requirements.  Who will carry on your family name?    Decorate Joseph's tag with a hammer.

THURSDAY:  Discuss what you feel the first Christmas gift was. The answer could be love, Jesus or Salvation? God so loved the world He sent His son so we might have eternal life. The answer could be all three. Read Luke 2: 4-5.

FRIDAY: Explain   Mary and Joseph were Jewish and celebrated **Hanukkah.** Each year it is on a different date near Christmas.  It is a time to offer thanks for the lights by lighting a candle in a candle holder called a Menorah each night.  This is a  holder with nine candles.  One candle called a servant candle is in the middle of the other eight.  It is used to light the eight candles during the eight days of Hanukkah.  Discuss what you know about this Jewish holiday.

SATURDAY: Read Matthew 2:6-7 and Luke 2: 7-20.  The angels coming to the shepherds was like being invited to the greatest birthday party of all times.

58

Luke 2: 20 tells the shepherds went back praising God. They were the first **witnesses** to spread the word. Think of how the news of Jesus is spread now.

## THE FOURTH WEEK IN ADVENT

SUNDAY: Light the fourth candle and give the last new figure to your teen. Each year there is a different number of days from now until Christmas, in which to discuss these topics. Pick one topic for each day left.

1. Read Luke 2: 21-28. When Jesus was presented at the temple, his parents offered **two turtle doves**. We know Jesus was born into a poor family because rich families brought lambs. Discuss how you help the poor.

2. Read Luke 2: 29-32. This is called the **Nunc Dimittis**. It means "let your servant go" from the opening words of Simeon. He says," my eyes have seen thy salvation". Explain that his eyes were looking at baby Jesus who is the Salvation of the world. The Nunc Dimittis is said in many churches.

3. Matthew 2:11 tells us the Wise Men found the child Jesus in a house. Discuss why Jesus wouldn't still be in the stable. Herod thought he was two.

4 Read Matt. 2:13-15. Although Jesus was Asian-born, he became a refugee in Africa. Discuss how this would help Jesus identify with the many who had to move because of tornadoes, famine, floods, hurricanes and other natural disasters. Think how you can help someone this Christmas.

5. Read all the paper strips that were placed in the manger for Jesus' bed.

6. Memorize part of " The Night Before Christ's Birth " in Chapter 11.

**CHRISTMAS EVE:** Read "The Night Before Christ's Birth. May your children's greatest thought on this Eve be of the manger that awaited Jesus at Midnight. May they feel the excitement knowing, when they awake, Jesus will be there.

**TWELVE DAYS OF CHRISTMAS:** On Christmas morning, read the chapter on Christmas to be reminded of things which make Christmas worthwhile. It is not our gifts, it's Baby Jesus. Move the shepherds to visit Jesus. Put white candles in the Advent Wreath. Pass out candy canes and remind everyone about the true meaning of them and a wreath.

The three small stripes show the marks of the scourging Jesus received. The white strip to symbolize the virgin birth. The hardness to symbolize the solid rock of our faith. The large red strip is for the blood shed by Jesus on the cross. Upside down the "J " for Jesus.

Our wreath means God has no beginning and no end. God is the Alpha and the Omega

**EPIPHANY:** The twelfth day after Christmas celebrates the visit of the Wise Men who were Gentiles and may have been the first non-Jewish visitors.

## CHAPTER 5

## JUST AS THE TWIG WAS BENT, THE TREE INCLINED
### Young Married Adults Start a Tradition

Each young family should start a special tradition to hand down from generation to generation. Parents need skills and a better understanding of how to honor Jesus and have fun at Christmas. To be truly effective, parents must first learn the Old and New Testament stories which correspond with each other telling about Jesus' birth. We'd like to share with you the following version of how we celebrate Christmas. Forty years ago our tradition started like the program in Chapter One. Now it's the culmination of Chapters One thru Four. We hope this chapter will help you understand the fundamentals of this tradition before you start your children in the program in Chapter One.

**FIRST WEEK IN ADVENT**

**SUNDAY:** We set up our Nativity and light the first candle in our Advent wreath. We make a pact to read a line or two from the Bible every day of the week at dinner time and move our Nativity figures to go with the reading.

**MONDAY:** We start the narrative from **Luke 1: 5.** "During the time Herod was King of Judea, there was a priest named Zachariah, who belonged to the priestly order of Abiajh. His wife's name was Elizabeth; she also belonged to a priestly family. They both lived good lives in God's sight and obeyed fully all the Lord's laws and commands. They had no children because Elizabeth was barren and she and Zachariah were both very old."

We start in the first chapter of Luke because it introduces the fulfilled prophecy saying the Messiah would have a forerunner. It's going to be John the Baptist, Zachariah's son.

**TUESDAY: We read Luke1:8-14.**    "One day Zachariah was doing his work as a priest in the Temple, taking his turn in the daily service. According to the custom followed by the priests, he was chosen by lot to burn incense on the altar. So he went into the Temple of the Lord. The crowd of people pray- ed outside during the hour when the incense was burned. An angel of the Lord appeared standing at the right side of the altar where the incense was burned. When Zachariah saw him, he was alarmed and felt afraid." But the angel said to him, "Don't be afraid Zachariah, God has heard your prayers, and your wife Elizabeth will bear you a son. You are to name him John."

We start our action here with a figure of an angel telling Zachariah his wife is going to have a baby.

**WEDNESDAY: We read Luke1:15-18.**    "How glad and happy you will be, and how happy many others will be when he is born. He will be a great man in the Lord's sight. He must not drink any wine or strong drink. From his very birth he will be filled with the Holy Spirit and he will bring back many of the people of Israel to the Lord their God. He will go ahead of the Lord, strong and mighty like the prophet Elijah. He will bring fathers and children together again; he will turn the disobedient people back to the way of thinking of the righteous; he will get the Lord's people ready for Him.' Zachariah said to the angel. 'How shall I know this is so? I am an old man, and my wife is old ' "

We ask are we ready to have God answer our prayers ? As a man of

God, Zach had been praying a long time for this to happen. Yet, he didn't believe it.

**THURSDAY: We read Luke1:19-20.** "I am Gabriel," the angel answered. "I stand in the presence of God, who sent me to speak to you and tell you the good news. But you have not believed my message, which will come true at the right time. Because you have not believed, you will not be able to speak; you will remain silent until the day my promise to you comes true."

We turn the figure of Zachariah to face the angel and tell him that he doubts him. Then we have the angel tell Zach because of his disbelief, he won't be able to talk until the proper time.

**FRIDAY: We read Luke1:21-22.** "In the meantime, the people were waiting for Zachariah and wondering why he was spending so much time in the Temple. When he came out, he could not speak to them. Then they knew that he had seen a vision in the Temple. Unable to say a word, he made signs to them with his hands."

We move Zach out of the Temple into the crowd. We have village people standing outside. At this point we do sign language. See Chapter 4.

**SATURDAY: We read Luke1: 23-25.** "When his period of service in the Temple was over, Zachariah went back home. Some time later his wife, Elizabeth, became pregnant and did not leave the house for five months. 'Now at last the Lord has helped me,' she said, 'He has taken away my public disgrace.' "

When Zachariah is finished in the Temple, we move Zach to his home with Elizabeth. We were excited when we finally found a house for Elizabeth.

## SECOND WEEK IN ADVENT

**SUNDAY:** We light the second candle in the Advent wreath. When we had only four nativity pieces, we started here reading **Luke 2** instead of Luke1:5. Before we bought a stable, we enjoyed a family project of making a gingerbread stable (Picture on page 78). **Directions for a gingerbread stable:**

1. Buy Sunshine cinnamon graham crackers that break into long strips and a package of coconut marshmallows ( they are light brown ).

2. Empty a 12 pack Pepsi carton. Make the space, where the cans are removed wider by bending the cardboard back two inches. This gives the carton (soon to be stable ) the appearance of doors.

3. Place carton on bottom of large pizza box. This will be used to carry the stable. Cut top of pizza box to cover the top and sides of carton to add strength. Glue together.

4. Put frosting on sides of stable. Press 3 and I/2 crackers into the frosting on each side. A single strip will be needed to be pressed on the front door.

5. Put frosting on the top of stable. Press on chex cereal for small tiles or bite size shredded wheat for large tiles.

6. At the corners, press one Rold Gold pretzel stick into frosting.

7. Use plain back side of graham crackers for road in front of stable.

8. Between doors lay one cracker. On it put two marshmallows for a manger.

9. Put coconut flakes in a dish and add green food coloring. After it dries, use it for grass around the stable. Add more coconut marshmallows to represent bales of straw for the animals.

9. Set out camels, donkeys and cows from a box of animal crackers.

10. Make palm trees out of pretzels adding green paper leaves on the top

**MONDAY: We read Luke1: 26-28.** "In the sixth month of Elizabeth's pregnancy God sent the angel Gabriel to a town in Galilee named Nazareth. He had a message for a girl promised in marriage to a man named Joseph, who was a descendant of King David. The girl's name was Mary. The angel said, 'Peace be with you. The Lord is with you and has greatly blessed you!' "

<u>We hold an angel near Mary to give her this message.</u>

**TUESDAY: We read Luke1:29-33.** "Mary was deeply troubled by the angel's message, and she wondered what his words meant. The angel said to her, ' Don't be afraid, ' Mary; God has been gracious to you. You will become pregnant and give birth to a son, and you will call him Jesus. He will be great and will be called the Son of the Most High God. The Lord God will make Him a king, as his ancestor David was, and he will be king of the descendants of Jacob forever; his kingdom will never end! ' "

<u>Now, we put Jesse lying at the base of the bare Jesse tree.</u>

**WEDNESDAY: We review** information about the Jesse Tree in Chapter 4.

**THURSDAY: We read Luke1:34-37.** "Mary said to the angel, 'I am a virgin. How, then can this be?' The angel answered, ' The Holy Spirit will come on you, and God's power will rest upon you. For this reason the holy child will be called the Son of God. Remember your relative Elizabeth? It is said that she cannot have children, but she herself is now six months pregnant, even though she is very old. For there is nothing that God cannot do.' ”

We add Mary's name to the Jesse tree. We couldn't find a male angel to represent Gabriel when the children were young. So we bought one in a blue dress. It is stilled used today

.

**FRIDAY: We read Luke 1: 38.** “ 'I am the Lord's servant,' said Mary; ' may it happen to me as you have said.' And the angel left her."

We discuss how Mary believed Gabriel quicker than Zachariah, a man of God. Mary took the news with acquiescence whether it was for shame or glory. Would we have believed the angel if we had been Mary ?

**SATURDAY: We read Luke 1: 39.** “A few days later Mary hurried to the highlands of Judea to the town where Zachariah lived, to visit Elizabeth.”

We put Mary on a donkey and take her to Elizabeth's house.

**THIRD WEEK IN ADVENT**
**SUNDAY;** We light the pink candle in the Advent Wreath which is used to denote joy. We sing the following song to the tune of "Jingle Bells":

Advent  bells, Advent Bell
telling all today
The joyful news that Jesus' birth
is well on it's way, yea.

Good News bells, Good News bells

Mary & Joseph on their way

to have Jesus in    Bethlehem,

His birth will be called Christmas Day.


**MONDAY: We read Luke 1: 41-55.** "At the sound of Mary's greeting, Elizabeth's child leaped within her and she was filled with the Holy Spirit. She gave a glad cry and exclaimed to Mary, ' Blessed art  thou among women and blessed is the fruit of thy womb.  And whence is this to me, that the mother of my Lord should come to me?  For, lo, as soon as the voice of thy salutation sounded in mine ears, the babe leaped in my womb for joy.   And blessed is she that believed: for there shall be a performance of those things which were told  her from the Lord.'

And Mary said, ' My soul doth magnify the Lord, and my spirit hath rejoiced in God my Savior.  For he hath regarded the low estate of his hand-maiden: for lo behold, from henceforth all generations shall call me blessed. For he that is mighty hath done to me great things; and holy is his name.  And his mercy is on them that fear him from generation to generation.  He hath showed strength with his arm; he hath scattered the proud in the imagination of their hearts.  He has put down the mighty from their seats, and exalted them of low degree.  He has filled the hungry with good things; and the rich he has sent empty away.  He has helped his servant Israel, in remembrance of his mercy;  As he spoke to our fathers, to Abraham, and to his seed forever.' "


<u>We pretend Elizabeth is listening to Mary say the Magnificat.</u>


**TUESDAY: We read Luke 1: 56.**    "And Mary abode with her about three months, and returned to her own house."

We leave Mary with Elizabeth a symbolic three days, instead of three months. Then we carry Mary back to her home in Galilee and place her in a house with her mother, Anna, and father, Heli. We then add Heli to the Jesse Tree.

**WEDNESDAY: We read Luke 1: 57-66.** "Now Elizabeth's full time came for her to be delivered, and she gave birth to a son. When her neighbors and relatives heard how the Lord had shown great mercy to her, they rejoiced with her. So it was, on the eighth day, that they came to circumcise the child; and they would have called him by the name of his father, Zachariah. His mother answered and said, ' No, he shall be called John.' But they said to her, 'there is no one among your relatives who is called by this name.' So they made signs to his father, what he would have him called. He signed for a writing tablet, and wrote, saying, ' His name is John.' So they all marveled. Immediately his mouth was opened and his tongue loosed, and he spoke, praising God. Then fear came on all who dwelt around them; and all these sayings were discussed throughout all the hill country of Judea. And all those who heard them kept them in their hearts, saying, ' What kind of child will this be ?' And the hand of the Lord was with Him."

We tape a cardboard tablet to Zach's hand with the words, "His name is John," printed on it.

**THURSDAY: We read LUKE 1: 67-80.** "Now John's father, Zachariah, was filled with the Holy spirit and prophesied saying: 'Blessed is the Lord God of Israel. For He has visited and redeemed His people, And has raised up a horn of salvation for us in the house of His servant David. As He spoke by the mouth of His holy prophets. Who have been since the world began, that we should be saved from our enemies.  And from the hand of all that hate us to perform mercy promised to our fathers.  And to remember His holy covenant. The oath which He swore to our father Abraham: To grant us that we, being delivered from the hand of our enemies, might serve Him without fear, in holiness and righteousness before Him all the days of our life.  And you, child will be called the prophet of the Highest:  For you will go before the face of the Lord to prepare His ways, to give knowledge of salvation to His people by the remission of their sins.  Through the tender mercy of our God, with which the Dayspring from on high has visited us; to give light to those who sit in darkness and the shadow of death, to guide our feet into the path of peace.' "

<u>We put Elizabeth and Zach back in their home and put John in a cradle.</u>

**FRIDAY: We read Luke 2:1.** "And it came to pass in those days that a decree went out from Caesar Augustus that all the world should be registered. This census  first took place while Quirinius was governing Syria.  So all went to be registered everyone to his own city."

<u>We set out Caesar Augustus, Quirinius and a Census taker.  When we couldn't  find a census taker  we took the lantern out of the innkeeper's hand and replaced it with names on a census list.</u>

**SATURDAY: We read Luke 2: 4-5.** "Joseph  also went up from Galilee out of the city of Nazareth, into Judea, to the city of David, which is called Bethlehem, because he was of the house and lineage of David, to be registered with Mary, his betrothed wife, who was with child."

69

We add Joseph's and David's names to the Jesse Tree. To insure think-ing of Jesus every day we put a piece of straw in the manger every time we tell the story or do a good deed. This tradition assures us when Christ is born, he'll have a nice soft bed as our gift of love to him.

## FOURTH WEEK IN ADVENT

**SUNDAY:** We light the fourth candle on the Advent wreath. We put our stable on the south side of our room and put Mary and Joseph on the north. Today, we start moving them south. We now begin one of the most change-able and interesting part of our little drama. We get out the map and try to decide the way Mary and Joseph should go to Bethlehem. Using a school map which takes up the whole wall. We put in pins to show where they are each day. At the same time, we make each table in the room a different town with people on it. To keep the tables from getting scratched we put green felt on them to represent grass.

**MONDAY:** The Bible doesn't tell how they went, therefore, we come up with our own theories. We check on how many days are left until Christmas and pick the route with the same number of days. Since Mary was pregnant, we might take the shortest route and go through Nain, Sychar, Shechem, Jacob's Well in Samaria, Bethel, Jerusalem and finally to Bethlehem. We might decide to go over to Dor and down though Lydia. A well traveled highway called Via Maris is there. As you can imagine, we learned some new geography each year. Our granddaughter, when she was five, could tell you the seven towns Mary would travel through. Sometimes, we pick famous places like Jacob's Well. Then we'd have a challenge to find a quantity of pitchers and women to put around it. Often we'd pick names like Michmash because of their sound.

**TUESDAY THROUGH SUNDAY:** Move the Holy Family each day south.

**CHRISTMAS EVE:** When our children were teenagers, our family started serving hot chocolate to people who came to the midnight service at St. Mark's in Grand Rapids. The tradition was carried on by others when we moved a-way. Now our children are married. We still try and meet at a church for the midnight service, and then come back to our house for cocoa.

Then we play the "Knock, Knock" game. The children like to act out Luke 2:4-7. We all sit around in the living room. We discuss how terrifying it might have been for Mary if she was wracked with labor pains. We discuss if Joseph might have felt inadequate as a protector or worried about Mary. The children carry Mary and Joseph to each person and pretend to **knock** on their door and ask for a room at their inn. Each person tells what has been important to them that year by the answer they give and why they have no room. Answers might be: "I'm sorry I only have room for my family." or "Sorry we have a golfer's group here." All inns are full except when we get to my dad. He'd always forget to say "No room." He'd always say, "Come on in."

Next we read "It Was The Night Before Christ's Birth" in Chapter 11. When the children were young and tucked in bed, we'd put up the Christmas tree, consequently Christmas Day would be more festive. Inasmuch as our tree cost as much as some of the finest gifts under it, we wanted it to be part of the Christmas surprise and keep it up the twelve days of Christmas. However, now our children are older and we select and cut the tree together. Another tradition is every year, we exchange ornaments with special friends. Then as we hang their ornament on the tree, we call out their name and say a prayer for them.

**CHRISTMAS DAY:** No presents are unwrapped until Jesus is in the manger. Therefore, we first check to see if Jesus is there. Then we check if presents are under the tree. We always asked the question, "If it's Jesus' birthday, why do we get the gifts?" The answer is always the same, "Because we have Jesus down in our heart." Then after each person opened one gift, we read Luke 2:6

"So it was, that while they were there, the days were completed for her to be delivered, and she wrapped Him in swaddling cloths, and laid Him in a manger, because there was no room for them in the inn."

As we think about Mary wrapping her baby, we take turns letting one person at a time unwrap their gift. Children thank the person who gave them the gift before they use it. Then they open another gift. Later, we add a white candle to the middle of the Advent wreath. For supper we have Jesus' birthday cake and sing "Happy Birthday dear, Jesus".

**Second day of Christmas we read Luke 2:8 -15.** "Now there were in the same country shepherds living out in the fields, keeping watch over their flock by night. And behold, an angel of the Lord stood before them, and the glory of the Lord shone around them, and they were greatly afraid. Then the angel said to them, 'Do not be afraid, for behold, I bring you good tidings of great joy which will be to all people. For there is born to you this day in the city of David a Savior, who is Christ the Lord. And this will be the sign to you: You will find a Babe wrapped in swaddling cloths, lying in a manger.' Then suddenly there was with the angel a multitude of the heavenly host praising God and saying: ' Glory to God in the highest, and on earth peace, goodwill toward men.' "

We tie angels on our tree. Then we move the shepherds under the tree. Now our grandchildren can visualize how awesome it was for the shepherds to look up and see the angels on high. How overwhelming it must have been.

**Third day of Christmas, we read Luke 2:15**. "So it was, when the angels had gone away from them into heaven, that the shepherds said to one another, 'Let us now go to Bethlehem and see this thing that has come to pass, which the Lord has made known to us.'

The angel's announcement to the shepherds accented Jesus' role as the good shepherd who would sacrifice his life for mankind. We put many candy canes representing the shepherd's staff on our tree. When the children act like good shepherds, they may have a candy cane but first they have to tell the six reasons for it (They are in the glossary).

**Fourth day, we read Luke 2: 16-20**. " And they made haste and found Mary and Joseph, and the Babe lying in a manger. And when they saw him they made known the saying which had been told them concerning this child; and all who heard it wondered at what the shepherds told them. But Mary kept all these things, pondering them in her heart. And the shepherds returned, glorifying and praising God for all they had heard and seen."

We move shepherds back to the hills of Judea.

**Fifth day we read Matthew 2: 1-2**. "Now when Jesus was born in Bethlehem of Judea in the days of King Herod, behold Wise Men from the East came to Jerusalem, saying 'Where is he that is born King of the Jews ?

For we have seen his star in the East and have come to worship him.' "

_We put the Wise Men with King Herod, in his palace._

**Sixth day we read Matthew 2:3-4.** "When Herod, the king, heard this, he was troubled, and all Jerusalem with him; and assembling all the chief priests and scribes of the people, he inquired of them where the Christ was to born."

_We couldn't find any scribes wearing skull caps called yarmulke. So, we painted black caps on some figures and placed them around King Herod._

**Seventh day we read Matthew 2:5-6.** "They told him ( King Herod ), 'In Bethlehem of Judea ( Christ would be born); for so it was written by the prophet: 'And you, O Bethlehem, in the land of Judea, are by no means least among the rulers of Judah; for from you shall come a ruler who will govern my people Israel.' Then King Herod summoned the Wise Men secretly and ascertained from them what time the star appeared; and he sent them to Bethlehem saying, ' Go and search diligently for the child, and when you have found him bring me word, that I too may come and worship him.' "

_The next five days we move the kings closer to Bethlehem._

**The eighth day of Christmas ( known to the world as New Year's Day) we read Luke 1: 21.** "And when eight days were completed for the circumcision of the Child, His name was called Jesus, the name given by the angel before He was conceived in the womb."

_We just have fun on Jesus' name day with hats and horns._

**The ninth day, we read Luke 2:22-24a.** "Now when the days of her purification according to the law of Moses were completed, they brought Him to Jerusalem to present Him to the Lord (as written in the law of the Lord), 'Every male who opens the womb shall be called holy to the Lord and to offer a sacrifice according to what is said in the law of the Lord,' "

_In order to be carried to the temple, we hooked Jesus on Mary's arm_

**The tenth day, we read Luke 2: 24b-28.** " Offer a pair of turtle doves or two young pigeons."

_Now Joseph carries the doves and Mary carries Jesus to the temple._

**The Eleventh day, we read Luke 2: 25-35.** " Now there was a man in Jerusalem, whose name was Simeon, and this man was righteous and devout, looking for the consolation of Israel, and the Holy Spirit was upon him. And it was revealed to him by the Holy Spirit that he would not see death before he had seen the Lord's Christ. Inspired by the Spirit he came into the temple; and when the parents brought in the child Jesus, to do for him according to the custom of the law, he took him up in his arms and blessed God and said, ' Now let thou servant depart in peace, according to thy word; for mine eyes have seen thy salvation which thou has prepared in the presence of all peoples, a light for revelation to the Gentiles, and for the glory of thy people Israel.' And his parents marveled at what was said about him; and Simeon blessed them and said to Mary, 'Behold, this child is set for the fall and rising of many in Israel, and for a sign that is spoken against (and a sword will pierce through your own soul also), that thoughts out of many hearts may be revealed.' "

We move Jesus and Joseph into the court yard next to Simeon.

**On the twelfth day read Luke 2:36-38.** "Now there was one, Anna, a prophetess, the daughter of Phanuel, of the tribe of Asher. She was of a great age, and had lived with a husband seven years from her virginity and this woman was a widow of about eighty-four years, and who did not depart from the temple but served God with fasting and prayers night and day. And coming in that instant she gave thanks to the Lord, and spoke of Him to all those who looked for redemption in Jerusalem."

We put Anna in a court yard outside the temple, where women are allowed. Simeon is in a different part. We have Mary and Joseph leave the doves and go back to Bethlehem to stay in a house.

**Christmas is over and it's now Epiphany. We read Matthew 2:9-12.** "When they heard the king, they departed; and behold the star which they had seen in the East went before them, till it came and stood over where the young Child was. When they saw the star, they rejoiced with exceedingly great joy. And when they had come into the house, they saw the young Child with Mary his mother, and fell down and worshipped Him. And when they had opened their treasures, they presented gifts to Him: gold, frankincense, and myrrh."

We have the Wise Men arrive on Epiphany, the 6th of January. We have an Epiphany party and cake. Read how in Chapter 13. When the Wise Men arrive we place the Holy Family in a house. They wouldn't have stayed very long in a stable. We put in a larger Jesus since he's now a child.

**Read Matthew 2:12-15.** "Then, being divinely warned in a dream they should not return to Herod, they departed for their own country another way. Now when they departed, behold, an angel of the Lord appeared to Joseph in a dream, saying, 'Arise, take the young Child and His mother, flee to Egypt, and stay there until I bring you word; for Herod will seek the young Child to destroy Him.' When he arose, he took the young Child and His mother by night and departed for Egypt, and was there until the death of Herod, that it might be fulfilled which was spoken by the prophet, saying, 'Out of Egypt will I call My Son.' "

Now the Christmas story is over. We take down our tree and put away our Nativity sets. We have the children order their figures for the next year.

Directions for making this Gingerbread Stable are on page 64. People are made out of bread dough and food coloring. Animals can be from a box of animal crackers. People can be cut from Christmas cards and folded back on sides to stand up.

# CHAPTER 6

## THE WORD WAS MADE FLESH AND DWELT AMONG US.   JOHN 1:14

### Adults 55+ Perceive Seeing is Believing

May this chapter give you insights to enable you to see the busy "traditions" you use in Advent in a different light.   At 55 plus years, our children are grown.   Now is the time to enjoy grandchildren and to help them see the Christmas Story in a different light.   Start the story: "Once upon a time God loved us so much that He sent us a wonderful Christmas gift.   It was the first Christmas gift the world had ever known.   In fact, before this gift arrived, there had never been a Christmas.   What was this special present?   It was Jesus.   He was wrapped in swaddling clothes."   Read the Christmas Story in your Bible, focus on how people today   recall   the wonderful story.

As   I started this chapter, it brought to mind, the 55+ Group from Faith Reform Church.   After they toured our home, they sat around the refreshment table and discussed how they could pass on the teachings of Christmas to their grandchildren.   One man remarked the new insights he had received made the round trip of sixty miles worthwhile.   Hope you feel the same !

*Luke 2:1    And it came to pass in those days.*

**Those days before Christmas** can be very challenging times.   It's a time when grandparents have the opportunity to do things they couldn't afford to do or didn't have the time to do as parents.   Now, they can help their family see Jesus as they prepare for Christmas.   They can pass on their knowledge in person or through letters.

*Luke 2:1      a decree went out from Caesar Augustus*

**When you receive Christmas cards** early, are you surprised the season is already here.  Caesar's decree was a surprise also to Mary and Joseph.  They were not as happy to hear from someone far away as we would be.  God's preparation for the first Christmas was a surprise to those who hadn't studied the scriptures.  As you receive cards, display the ones which focus on Jesus.

*Luke 2: 3      everyone into their own city.*

**When shopping in the city** is it exciting or drudgery?   Is buying gifts an obligation or a privilege?  How do you think the Holy Family felt about bring-ing  their gift to the world?  If you feel annoyed in a crowd, think of how Mary and Joseph felt.  Do you think they realized Jesus was sent for everyone pressing around them?  Give gifts to your grandchildren which will help them grow spiritually and increase their understanding of how important they are to you.  A gift of time, such as a coupon to take them fishing, bowling,  to a movie, or swimming, is ultimately showing them time together is very special because they are.  If you give a book include a note promising to read it to them.   Make a genuine grandparent connection.

*Luke 2: 4      which is called Bethlehem.*

**When baking,** remember in Hebrew, Bethlehem means a "house of bread".  Jesus called himself the "bread of life.   Jesus provided bread for the hungry and blessed bread giving us the Lord's supper. Does breaking bread, ever remind you of Jesus' broken body on the cross?  With whom can you share your daily bread?  Invite a lonely or hungry person for cookies. and tea. When baking with your grandchild, explain the pretzel is used as a symbol of children folding their arms when they go to the altar on Christmas to be blessed.  Make a gingerbread stable.  See illustration in Chapter Five.

*Luke 2:4    because He was of the house and lineage of David.*

**When you set up your tree**, think of your family tree and Jesus.  The Son of God was born into a human family.  Joseph was from the line of King David which had been given the promise that the Messiah would come through his family.  Now God was keeping His promise!   Ever faithful. (Evergreen).  Take advantage of this time to share your grandchild's baby book and talk to them how joyful you were at their birth and how blessed Mary must have felt giving birth to Jesus.  To document the family's lineage buy a Grandmother Book or using its guidelines write your own book.  Mention persons in your family who have transmitted the true spirit of Christmas.

*Luke 2:6    Mary brought    forth her firstborn Son*

**When you bring forth the presents** reflect about the reason why gifts are given.  How many gifts are really necessary?  Remember the gift of a Savior was truly necessary for our salvation.   Do gifts remind you of God's gift?.....Jesus!!  When you receive a gift, reflect on how you receive Jesus and His love.  Contemplate about how exhausted Mary was as she laid Jesus in the manger.  Then guide your grandchild to understand a gift of self, not money, is a greater gift, (like ten hugs or a promise to write three letters).

Set an example of giving a gift of time to your children. In the form of an I.O.U. volunteer to run errands or take your grandchildren to appointments. This lets your children know they aren't burdening you with their problems.

*Luke 2: 7a     And she wrapped Him in swaddling cloth.*

**As you wrap gifts,** think of how Mary wrapped Jesus in swaddling bands. Sometimes wrappings look great and we don't appreciate what's inside. Some people get into the "wrappings of Christmas" and fail to see what God wrapped for us, in flesh and blood. Jesus was wrapped in human form. Buy wrappings which honor Jesus. Let the children make paper with angels. Write on your tags "Blessings on Jesus' birth" or "Have a great day on His birth."

*Luke  2: 7b    and laid Him in a manger*

**As you enjoy the aroma of Christmas** (pine, candles, a turkey roasting), think of how the first Christmas smelled. Odors make things real. Ask the children what they think the manger or stable smelled like! To help them know what Mary's gifts smelled like, buy some frankincense or oil of myrrh .

*Luke 2: 7c     there was no room for them*

**As your guests arrive,** receive them as if they were Jesus. "For as you did it to one of the least of these my brethren, you did it to me." Remember, Jesus comes into our home and hearts like a guest. Do your Christmas activities make Jesus feel welcomed? God welcomes you into His heavenly home and gives you eternal life through Jesus.

*Luke 2: 7d     in the inn*

**As you eat or drink something "seasonal" in your inn,** remember the hospitality of the inn was denied to the Holy family. Think of someone who would otherwise be alone. Allow your grandchild to bring a friend over. Be a good listener. Ask questions about their holiday.

*Luke 2: 8     There were shepherds abiding in the field*

**When you set up your Advent Wreath and light the candles** (often made of beeswax ) abide with your family but don't get as busy as a bee and forget to include Jesus. Even the shepherds left their work to honor Jesus.

*Luke 2: 9b     and the glory of the Lord shone around them,*

**When you put up outside lights and decorations,** may the beauty outside be a reflection of the love within and remind people of Jesus" birth. The outdoor display the shepherds saw really got their attention for the purpose of directing them to the Babe in the manger.

*Luke 2: 10     ... tidings of great joy, which shall be to all people.*

**When you give to a charity,** think about the connection between Jesus' birth and helping people. Do you think God can see a correlation between His gift of eternal life and our gifts. Is love and joy in our giving? Help a child make a place mat out of Christmas cards and then let them experience the joy of taking it to someone in a Nursing Home.

*Luke 2: 11   "....a Savior which is Christ the Lord*

**When you read Jesus' precious name which is so familiar** in the Christmas story, do you savor the words of Scripture as a sacred moment. Visualize "the word was made flesh and dwelt among us."   Give a Bible or a Christmas Story Book as a gift.   Explain to your grandchild, Jesus means, "the Lord is Salvation."   Discuss the real meanings of the names you received at baptism and devise affectionate names to call each other.   Think of other special names for Jesus.

*Luke 2:12    And this shall be a sign unto you....*

**When you see snow,** it should be a sign to remind you that everything comes from God.   When snow falls and everything is white, people in the north start singing,  "It's beginning to look a lot like Christmas."   We should sing it's beginning to look like Christmas when Mary enters the stable.   There probably wasn't snow in that region the night Jesus was born.   Yet, snow in the Bible is a sign of God's forgiveness: "Wash me, and I shall be whiter than snow," (Ps. 51: 7). "Though your sins be as scarlet, they shall be as white as snow," (Is. 1: 18) and "My word is like snow covering the earth"  (Is. 55:18). Teach your grandchildren how to make a snow angel by having them lie on new snow and move just their arms and legs back and forth.

*Luke 2: 13    a multitude of the heavenly host praising God*

**When you go to a Christmas program and hear the multitude** praising God, think of how beautiful it is when the Lord's people sing together. We should work together to the Glory of God all year. Remember to sing "Happy Birthday" to Jesus as he is placed in the manger on Christmas morn. Learn the real meaning of the song, " The Twelve Days of Christmas."

*Luke 2: 14    Glory to God in the highest.*

**When you play, sing, or listen to heavenly music** at Christmas remember the background of the songs and where some of them come from in the Bible. The Magnificat of Mary, (Luke 1: 46-54) the Benedictus of Zacharias, (Luke 1: 68-79) and the Nunc Dimittis of Simeon, (Luke 2: 29-35) and the Glory in Excelsis of the angels (Luke 2:14). They all tell the story of Jesus' birth, yet they are sung all year in many churches.

*Luke 2: 16    and they found Mary and Joseph with the Babe.*

**When you find and unpack your ornaments,** many special memories will be attached. We have forgotten many of them until we open the boxes and are ready to use them. The Christmas story is like ornaments. Its been in the Bible all the time but now, during Advent, some find Mary, Joseph and the Babe for the first time through these symbols. God's love is just waiting to be used. Buy or make a loving Christian ornament for your grandchild to hang on the tree. If dated and signed with, "I love you," it will always remind him, he is special to God and to you.

*Luke 2: 17a    And when they had seen Him*

**When you see Jesus in the manger,** do you feel that Jesus is the greatest gift of all!  What do you think Mary and Joseph said when they saw Jesus?

*Luke 2: 17b    they made known abroad the saying about this child.*

**When sending Christmas cards,** it's our way of proclaiming Jesus' birth. The shepherds found a way of sharing the good news.  We can, too by using religious postage stamps and cards.  We can pray for each person as we write their address and enclose a note expressing how God's love has made a difference in our life.  We can write to let our children and grandchildren know they are special and are cherished, loved, and adored by us and Jesus.

*Luke 2: 18    ...and all they that heard it wondered at those things....*

**When carolers come to your house,** the joy is contagious.  The shepherds were not professional story tellers, yet they were able to share what they had seen and heard.  Think of how you can "repeat the sounding joy" by making room for Jesus.

*Luke 2: 19a    But Mary kept all these things....*

**When you keep something familiar** does it give you peace?   If you have ornaments with family members' pictures on them, pray for each person as you put their image on the tree.  Ask God to bless them with the peace which passes all understanding.  Remember Mary kept spiritual things in her heart not material things.

*Luke 2: 19b*     *.......and pondered them in her heart.*

**When you think about Christmases past**, ponder if Jesus fits in each scene. Thank God for those who made past Christmases so memorable. Pray for someone who is absent due to miles or circumstances. Remember Mary had a propensity to enjoy and ponder the simple gifts around her as well as the extraordinary occurrence of her son's birth.

*Luke 2: 20b*     *as it was told unto them.*

**When you go to church** do you feel it's another opportunity to hear His word? Do the extra Advent services remind you they are a favor God does for us to help the Holy Spirit rekindle our faith ?

*Matthew 2: 4*     *Herod demanded of them.*

**When hearing someone explain about the Christmas symbols**, are you gratified no one demands that information from you? Have a fun quiz on Jesus' birth. Give prizes shaped like bells or angels or pass out candy canes.

*Matthew 2: 8*     *He ordered, Go and search.*

**When you think about ordering things** for your grandchildren search for videos, books, computer software and Nintendo games about Jesus. Purchase a nativity set or items with Christian designs such as bowls, cups, potholders, stationery or a puzzle with an angel or Mary with Jesus.

*Matthew 2: 11 "When they opened their treasures"*

**When you display your outside treasure,** be sure it is Jesus. Buy or make an outdoor nativity set. My sister copied and enlarged a Christmas card on plywood of Mary and Joseph on a donkey. She moved it closer each day to the stable. One day it froze in the snow and couldn't be moved . They never made it to Bethlehem. Jesus in the manger had to be brought to them. The neighbors never stopped talking about the couple's hard journey.

*Matthew 2: 11b "they presented Him with gifts"*

**When you present people with gifts**, be creative about honoring Jesus. Make a needlepoint or cross-stitch nativity or a wooden for a dollhouse. Cut out a set on a jig saw or carve one. Be sure you put your name and the date on the back so your set can be handed down to the next generation. Put swaddling clothes on a baby doll or make a felt Advent calendar. Make love gifts out of old wrappings and bows. A love gift is a small empty package placed under the tree to give to visitors with the attached note:

This is a very special gift;

A gift for you and me.

The reason it's so special

Is because this gift is free.

This gift is very priceless,

A gift of God's great love.

You see, the gift is Jesus

Who was sent from God above.

Please keep this gift
and leave the ribbon tied.
Consider it a keepsake
From Jesus Christ who died.

May we always seek God's presence
Each and every day.
We hope this gift reminds you
He is the Truth, the Light, the Way.

Jesus came to give us life
and that's the reason why,
We serve Him with our special gifts
His name to glorify!!!

A felt Advent calendar with
an angel warning the Wise Men.

*Matthew 2: 11    Gold, frankincense and myrrh.*

**When you display gold, frankincense and myrrh on Epiphany,** you can be sure your grandchildren will tell all their friends they have seen the real substance.    Read Chapter Thirteen for ordering information.

*Matthew 2: 12    they departed into their own country*

**When Christmas is over, and everyone departs,** evaluate how you can honor Jesus more next year.    I hope you have learned different ways to look at Christmas. Tell your grandchildren, they will always be wise if they follow **Jesus.**

## CHAPTER 7

## GRANDPARENTS, TODAY'S WISE MEN
### Customs of our forefathers

Throughout the Bible old age and wisdom are honored. The early chapters of this book offer suggestions for starting new traditions. However, Christian ways of forefathers should be treasured. As head of your family you should be able to explain the customs of your forefathers which honored Jesus. If they didn't have any family traditions explore some from the land of your great grandparents. Some are listed at the end of this chapter. Don't celebrate the birth until Jesus is in the manger. Help spiritual growth to continue by learning something new each year about Jesus. Don't let "gift giving" and shopping get out of control. Instead use time to share why Jesus loved us enough to enter into our world.

Sadly today, many people from the Senior Center and Hospice groups remark Christmas is a lonely time for them. There seems to be no room for them in the inn. There is only room for children. They have difficulty finding a reason to get out of bed. If you or someone you love has this problem use the suggestions below. They are called anticipation envelopes. We used this idea when my mom was alone due to my dad's death.

My Mom lived in a city many hours away from me. Since I couldn't stay with her, I left her a packet of prepared envelopes. She was to open one a day. She told me, each morning she'd eagerly get up and, while having her coffee, open up an envelope to see her assignment for the day. My Mom told me how much she appreciated her packet giving her a plan and a lift for the day. These packets are a reminder God sent Jesus at Christmas time for all.

If your loved ones live far from you, prepare your anticipation notes from the ideas below. Be creative and add some new ideas. Put each one in a different envelope. Send enough for every day in December. Mail a packet to the one you love with the directions:

**Take one a day and call me some morning.        Dr. Love**

If you're a golden-ager, let the following tasks be your anticipation notes each day. You don't have to do them in order. You can put numbers 1 - 26 in a bag and then draw a number and do that numbered task. You can also think of the many people in the Christmas story mentioned in Matthew and Luke and pick one to emulate each day. Like the Wise Men follow the star (task ) placed before you.

**Tasks for the day for healthy golden agers:**

1. Set out the Advent Wreath. Put in the four candles.
2. Show how "great" you consider someone close to you. Do a job for them that they don't like to do. Leave a note signed by "Mary" or "Joseph."
3. Be a good innkeeper. Make room for someone at your dinner table or give a friend a certificate for dinner to be used when they feel lonely.
4. Make a gingerbread stable with a young child. See picture on page 78.
5. Bethlehem means "bread." Take a loaf of homemade bread to your police or fire station. Thank them for their willingness to work on "His" birthday.
6. Teach someone to knit, embroider, quilt, or cross-stitch. Put a Christmas sampler together for a homebound person.
7. Like the census taker, write down an accurate account of your life. Buy a Grandma's Book at Hallmark's to record it in. Give it as a gift to a grandchild.

8. For older children buy a loose-leaf notebook. Encourage them to write their own family history or to relive precious moments in their life.

9. Make angel cookies. Share them with a friend.

10. Baby sit a grandchild and organize your family photographs. Reconnect her/him to the past and reminisce about all the joy you've had together.

11. Invite single friends over to a cooking party. As your gift to them, teach them how to make one of your Christmas specialties.

12. We give gifts to those who have Jesus in their hearts since we can't give them directly to Him. You have shown your love for Jesus, do something special for yourself. Get your hair or nails done or buy your favorite food.

13. Be like Joseph, pass on your skills. For Advent give your grandchild her own tools as an early Christmas gift. Help her to use them to build a stable or do repairs for someone in need.

14. Give yourself another gift. Get a book from the library or sign up for a class about something which can improve your life.

15. Buy tapes or CDs made by Christian artists for a friend in a nursing home.

16. Like Joseph, take someone else's child under your wing. Look for a mother with children in your church. Ask her if she would like you to teach her child how to make Christmas goodies, at your house or hers.

17. Ask your minister for the names of three people who will be alone on Christmas. Invite them to a Christmas pot luck. Ask them if they would bring a dish to pass and a recipe which reminds them of a special time.

18. Be the census taker. Count your Santa decorations and those honoring Jesus. Be sure Jesus is the winner.

19. Take a poinsettia to someone in the nursing home. Tell them you brought the plant, because it looks like the star the Wise Men followed.

20 Display all your Christmas cards which honor Jesus.

21. Teach your grandchild about your religious heritage. Get out an old Bible. Go through the family tree and retell stories about their parents. Then for a surprise Christmas gift, wrap it and give it away in love.

22. In the name of Jesus, give a prized possession to someone special in your life. Give it to someone because God sent you His gift swaddled in linen.

23. Learn "T'Was the Night Before Christ's Birth." It is in Chapter Eleven.

24. Spend some money to call special friends to let them know you care.

25. Have a Merry Christmas with Jesus and some friends.

26. Make an Epiphany cake for friends. Directions are in Chapter 13.


**Tasks for bedridden scribes, shepherds and Marys.**

Some people are like Herod's scribes. They are good at writing things down. Some are like the shepherds who told everyone what happened. These people communicate well on the phone. Others are like Mary who pondered things in her heart. These Marys know how to proclaim to God through prayer their needs and the needs of others. Pick tasks which you can do.


Each day pray about, write to or make a phone call to one of these persons:

1. During Advent, light a candle for someone you know who has "switched off Jesus." Pray the light of Jesus be restored in their lives. When you turn off your light to go to bed, pray for others who haven't seen Jesus' light.

2. Pray you will be well prepared for Jesus' coming. Thank God and pray you won't waste the years you have left. Share the joy of His birth with those you see today. Pray for an older friend.

3. Be an angel (messenger), pray for/write/call a forgotten friend.

4.. Call/send a note to a college student who is being ridiculed for his beliefs. Give them a gift of "faith." Tell them how you know Jesus.

5. Pray for/ call/write a note of encouragement to a grandchild.

6. Pray for/ call/send a note to someone whose loved one died this year. Share your thoughts of how Jesus' birth gives one victory over death.

7. Read the Advent Chapter. Tell your friends what you have learned.

8. Pray for/ call/write someone who has cared for a sick relative and thank them for their Christian witness.

9. Get names and addresses of college students from your church and write them an Advent message.

10. Remember the message of Christmas is more important then the number of cards you send or get. Only send cards or notes which honor Jesus.

11. Give a tube of "Super glue" to a friend who has stuck by you through thick and thin. Let them know you appreciate their love and faithfulness.

12. Recall those who made Christmas special for you. Send them a "Medal of Christian Witness." Enclose a note telling how you saw the love of Jesus in their actions.

13. Give a word of praise to someone about their unique qualities. Many aren't told they are appreciated or special very often

14. Read Chapter Fifteen to learn about the journey Mary and Joseph took.

15. When you feel weak and frail, start counting things which appear weak but in actuality are quite strong (spider webs, silk threads, etc.) Baby Jesus' message continues to change the world.

16. Write or tell your pastor and his wife how much the taped sermons and their visits mean to you. Pray for them.

17. Be like Augustus, send out a decree (thank you note) for a job well done to the person who delivers your mail, the garbage collector or a church member or officer. Tell them to have a good day on Jesus' birthday.

18. Read the Prophecies in Chapter 9. Discuss them with your friends.

19. Pray for those who don't make room for Jesus. Remember, ignorance or deceit keeps Jesus in the stable.

20 When you think of those who are depressed because no one seems to remember them, remind them Jesus remembers them and loves them. Many of your great grand children also feel this pain when Santa brings the bully next door the gift they wanted but didn't get. Remember them.

21 Read Chapter Fourteen about angels. Rethink your beliefs about them.

22. Do something special for yourself today. Remember Jesus loves you.

23. As you think of the animals in the stable who shared their hay and milk, pray for the quiet workers in your church who are "silent witnesses."

24. Start a journal about your favorite Christmas to pass on to your children. Write down the Christmas customs your parents had or you had.

25. Say "Happy Jesus' Birthday" instead of Merry Christmas.

26. Day after Christmas, read Christmas Chapter Twelve and learn code for Twelve Days of Christmas. Share it with a friend.


## CUSTOMS OF OUR FOREFATHERS

If you don't see your grandparent's tradition listed below, write it down. My family made up their own. Yet, as we made up our traditions, we were surprised that other people around the world had similar customs which we thought were ours and ours alone. When you love and honor Jesus, you begin to think alike.


## AFRICA

The Christian Ethiopian, members of the Coptic Orthodox Church, celebrate Christmas on January 7th, with wise men bearing gifts.

## ALASKA

The children play "Going Around the star" by taking a large star from door to door by boys and girls. They are invited in for refreshments after singing carols. The second night of Christmas week the star bearers are followed by others (sometimes adults) who dress to represent Herod's soldiers, trying to capture the star and to destroy it as Herod's men tried to destroy baby Jesus.

## AMERICA/MAIN LAND

Christians put up their wreath and Nativity set and attend special church services through the four weeks of Advent. Christmas Eve, they put up their tree and go to a candlelight service at 11 p.m. Otherwise, they go on Christmas Day. Often the Messiah is sung and played on that night as a presentation of Christian theology. Everyone stands to the rousing chorus of "Hallelujah". Fruitcake is given as a remembrance of the Wise Men who carried fruits and nuts and dates to eat on their long journey. Carolers sing at homes or in institutions. Many give to the needy at Christmas. Many churches have Nativity programs. Homes are decorated with lights to remind us, "Jesus is the Light of the world." Some end the twelve days of Christmas by taking down the tree and decorations and putting away the Nativity set on Epiphany.

## AUSTRIA

"Showing the Christ Child" is a widespread nativity play where a manger is carried from house to house. Three young people are chosen to be the kings. Behind the kings, family after family join until they gather at the steps of the church. This country's contribution is "Silent Night! Holy Night! ".

## BELGIUM

Bells ring, then there is a procession and finally the people crowd into the church. Later, they have a home celebration. It is a custom for each village to appoint three men to be the Magi. They make their rounds and sing at each home. This is a Flander's tradition.

## BETHLEHEM

Christians throughout the world gather for midnight mass in the town where Jesus was born. They kneel to kiss the silver star set in the ground where it is believed Jesus was born.

## BULGARIA

Head of the house says, "Christ is born." Family responds "He is born indeed."

## COSTA RICA

A family has a large replica of the Nativity. The presepio fills a whole room. People go from house to house admiring them. These variations of "presepio" are known as the portal. The Christ Child is the main bearer of gifts not Santa.

## CZECHOSLOVAKIA ( FORMER-Now separated into Czech Republic and Republic of Slovakia )

At midnight, all get ready for the Holy Mass at church called Pasterka. The manger called "jeslicky" is never missing from a home or church.

## DOMINICAN REPUBLIC

Christmas remains a religious day. Children receive gifts on January 6th, Wise Men's day.

## ENGLAND ( medieval)

On Dec. 24th it was the custom to put out a Nativity tray which would bring the special night into sharp focus. Legend has it, on the night of the nativity, whoever ventures out and puts on this tray a bone for a lost hound, a wisp of hay for a shivering horse, a warm cloak for a stranded wayfarer, a dish of crumbs for all huddled birds and sweetmeats for little children, will be blessed with returned gifts which will rival the hues of the peacock. It's a night to think of others. On Christmas the Messiah is often sung and played in London since it is where Handel wrote it and his hometown. Everyone stands for the chorus of "Hallelujah," continuing a practice started by King George.

## FRANCE

Many families attend midnight mass and decorate their homes with small Nativity scenes. In these scenes, clay figures called santons (little saints) portray the story of Jesus' birth. Some people add new santons every year. They are sold at special holiday fairs. The stable contains small figurines including representations of Jesus, Mary, Joseph, shepherds, the cow, and a donkey. In some regions of the country the santons represent people of every day life as well as Biblical characters. People go to midnight mass and return home for supper, and a puppet show about the Christmas story.

## GERMANY

Churches are open the entire week before Christmas. Their custom is to add a paper star to their Advent wreath each Sunday. The stars have an Old Testament verse on one side and a New Testament verse on the opposite. These are to be memorized and discussed at home. To find appropriate verses for your star, read Chapter Nine on Prophecies to correlate the messages.

## GREAT BRITAIN

They have an Advent Wreath. On Christmas Eve they go to midnight service and then have a carol sing. No one sees the tree until 6 P.M. They decorate the tree after the children are in bed.

## GREECE

They have treats, such as Christpsomo (Christ bread ) after they return from Mass. They don't have Christmas trees. On Epiphany, they throw a cross into the water, thus bringing the season to a close. The village priest goes from house to house sprinkling holy water everywhere to bless the homes.

## HONDURAS

Christmas is preceded by nine days of seeking lodging for the Holy Family. A house in town is picked for the faithful to go to each of the nine nights saying prayers and singing hymns. The household receives a special blessing from the priest. Masses are held and most homes have Nativity scenes called Nacimientos.

## HUNGARY

Hungarians give the church, rather than the homes, a larger part in the observance of the anniversary of Christ's birth.

## IRELAND

The Irish place lighted candles in their windows as an invitation for Christ to find His way and guide those like Joseph & Mary who are seeking shelter.

## ITALY

Each year, families flock to Rome to buy Nativity arrangements which are called presepio. The figures are called pastori. The focal point, the Child, is placed in the manger by the mother on Christmas Eve, while everyone prays. All families try to afford a small presepio. More expensive ones include many animals---cows, horses, dogs. Small clay figurines in bright colors represent villagers at their daily chores. The carpenter swings a hammer, the miller carries a sack of grain, the peasant milks her long-haired goat. Guests kneel in front of it. At 9 P.M. all proceed to church. Each church seeks to exhibit the biggest and most artistic manger.

## JAPAN

The children sing carols and reenact the Nativity.

## LITHUANIA

They have a table with layers of straw in memory of the night in Bethlehem.

## MEXICO

The nine days before Christmas have special importance. These days are called posadas, which means resting place or inn. The home must be ready to receive friends by December 16th. the beginning of the posadas. On each day, Mexicans reenact Mary and Joseph's search for lodgings on the first Christmas Eve. They commemorate the hardships of Mary and Joseph. First, they erect an altar covered with pine branches and moss and a Nativity which has hills, huts, shepherds, a stable and a empty manger. Then families go to one another's homes and divide into two groups, one acting as the inn-keeper and the other, the Holy Family (Pilgrims). Each pilgrim receives a candle.

Two children, carrying figures of Mary and Joseph, lead a procession of people to a particular house. The procession marches through the house singing and asking for shelter. First they are refused but are finally admitted:

Pilgrims knock.

Innkeeper: Who knocks ?

Pilgrims: Pilgrims who need a place to rest.

Innkeeper: Find some other place. Don't disturb me.

Pilgrims: We're tired and hungry

Innkeeper: Who are you? I don't know you.

Pilgrims: Joseph of Nazareth and Mary my wife, who will be the mother of the Son of God.

Innkeeper: Then come in to my humble home. May the Lord give shelter to me when I leave this world.

Everyone goes into the living room and says prayers. Similar to:" O God, who is coming to save us, help us to never close our hearts when you are knocking." At the end of the evening a small image of Jesus is placed in the cradle on the altar and candles are lit around it and all join in singing "Alleluia, Alleluia! Let us rejoice because the Lord has come to His people! Let us sing praises to the Lord, Come you, sing and rejoice! Blessed is he that comes in the name of the Lord. Hosanna in the Highest!"

After the nine days, the whole family goes to mass on Christmas Eve. Christmas Day is quiet. Santa Claus and trees are rare.


NORTH AMERICA/ALBERTA/ SASKATCHEWAN

Ukrainian communities here maintain many of the traditions of their ancestral homeland. In honor of Christ's birth, some families observe a fast. They don't eat meat for six weeks before the Ukrainian Christmas, which is on January 7th.

On the 6th, Christmas Eve, the children stand outside to wait for the first star of the night. As soon as they see it, they run into their home and start their Christmas Eve festivities. Dinner consists of twelve meatless dishes in memory of the 12 apostles of Christ. Everyone must have at least one spoonful of each of the twelve dishes.

## NORWAY

Rings in Christmas (ringe in Julen) at 5 P.M. on Christmas Eve. Children are not allowed to see the tree until then. Gifts are received January 6th.

## PHILIPPINES

The Filipino attends Mass very early each morning the nine days before Christmas. It is called Misass de Gallo (Masses of the Cock). Christmas Eve is celebrated at midnight with Mass. Jesus' birthday is a great festival, ushered in by the ringing of the bells for hours and mass is held every hour so everyone can come. They have simple religious plays called pastores performed by young people who go from village to village portraying the Bible story.

## POLAND

People attend Pasterka (Shepherd's Mass) at midnight on Christmas Eve. Many follow the tradition by breaking an Oplatek, a thin wafer made of wheat flour and water. Nativity scenes are stamped on the Oplatek. The head of the house holds the wafer and each person breaks off and eats a small piece. It is similar to communion wafers.

## RUSSIA

It is customary to fast on Christmas Eve until after church service. Frequently they have the blessing of homes. A priest visits homes and sprinkles each room with holy water.

## SPAIN

People sing in the streets after Mass. Many homes and churches have Nacimiento, which are miniature Nativity scenes. They celebrate Epiphany after the twelve days of Christmas.

## SWEDEN

Special ceremonies and festivities are held on January 6 in honor of the Three Magi. Young people choose three among them to dress in costumes of the three kings. Then, following the kings, the young people form processions marching through the streets of the village. They sing special carols and carry a large " Star of Bethlehem " as their banner.

## SWITZERLAND

In many villages, children celebrate " Sternsingen"( shtern'-sing-en ), or "Star Singing ," with an elaborate pageant. Three are chosen to dress as the Kings. They march in a torch light procession, bearing their gifts to the manger scene, where others portray members of the Holy Family. Then those who are dressed like angels stand around the manger holding a great illuminated "Star of Bethlehem" on a pole.

**VENEZUELA** People go to Midnight Mass. Some receive gifts on Christmas Day, but many receive their gifts on Epiphany.

## CHAPTER 8

## FROM NAZARETH TO EGYPT

### Traveling with Mary and Joseph

Many non-Christian families teach their young children the names of Santa's seven reindeer. Christians can have as much fun learning the names of the seven towns the Holy Family may have traveled through on their way to Bethlehem. This chapter has been prepared in response to questions by friends about those towns. The decree of Caesar Augustus ordered people to be enrolled by going to the place of origin of their family. It was to make tax collecting easier by having their names on the rolls. However, God used Augustus. His decree caused the prophecy to be fulfilled which said the Messiah would be born in Bethlehem. The Bible doesn't give the route Mary and Joseph took to Bethlehem. So we must use our imagination. Our family varies the route from year to year.

The most direct route was more like a cattle path from Nazareth through Nain, to Sychar in the Samaria district. Then the water-parting Route started at 'Shechem. It went through Jacob's Well, Bethel, Michmash, Jerusalem and to Bethlehem. Being pregnant, Mary might have preferred the shortest route. Yet, the Jews had an aversion about Samaritans and their land.

Second choice was a network of roads crisscrossing the Holy Land developed by trade routes connecting the kingdoms of Egypt, Mesopotamia, and Asia Minor. There were two important arteries. The King's Highway, went north to south through Palestine. The coastal route, the "way of the sea," was called Via Maris ( However, when the prophet Isaiah spoke of the "way of the sea," he was referring to the Sea of Galilee).

Mary and Joseph might have taken the Via Maris route. It would be longer but quicker and safer since people and caravans would give protection. The Coastal Route, the principal trade route crossing Palestine, at Mount Carmel, became one sector and ran southward to Egypt. Mary and Joseph may have gone west from Nazareth to area near Dorr . There they would connect with the Way of the Sea. Then they'd go through Caesarea and Joppa. Next, they'd connect to a lesser road crossing the Holy Land going east to Jerusalem.

A third route meandered near the River Jordan and wound like a snake through the valley. It went close to fishermen and farmers and then abandoned the Jordan for a safer area, near the foot of the hills. It was a dangerous route because of wild animals. Finally they would have reached the date groves of Jericho. Then they had to climb over a rocky area and go near a gorge, on their way to Jerusalem and finally Bethlehem.

## TAKING THE STRAIGHT ROUTE TO BETHLEHEM

Nazareth: The town in a secluded valley of lower Galilee where Mary and Joseph lived. Jerusalem was eighty miles by the direct route.

Nain : A town where Jesus raised to life the only son of a widow. Luke 7: 11

Samaria : The capital of the ten tribes of Israel. The Jews had a repugnance of any social and religious association with the Samaritans. The mountain districts were inhabited by people of mixed race descended from the remnants of the northern tribes and non-Israelites brought into the area after Samaria's fall. Prejudice caused many Jews to detour across the Jordan through Peraea. This capital city built on a hill was 5 1/2 miles NW of Shechem.

Jacob's well : An ancient well near Sychar, near the parcel of ground Jacob gave to his son, Joseph. Jesus talked to the women of Samaria there.

Shechem: The district of Samaria in the narrow pass between twin mountains.

Bethel: It means "house of God." It is south of Shiloh. In Gen.28:19 to 30: 13 Jacob called it Bethel because of the vision he saw there and erected a pillar to mark the spot. It's about 12 miles N of Jerusalem.

Michmash : A town three miles southeast of Bethel, and seven and a half miles north of Jerusalem (1 Sam. 13: 2).

Jerusalem : It was the sacred city. It was made the capital of the kingdom by David. It meant foundation of peace and a secure habitation to the Hebrews. Mary and Joseph will take Jesus and two turtle doves there after Jesus' birth.

Bethany : A small town near the Mt. of Olives, which means " House of Figs." Jesus often lodged there. The hometown of Lazarus, Mary and Martha. It was two miles from Jerusalem by way of a footpath.

Bethlehem : Birth place of David. It was looked to as the place the Messiah would be born (Mic. 5: 2, Matt. 2: 1). In its vicinity were the shepherds. It is five miles south of Jerusalem. Bethlehem means "House of Bread." This is interesting since this is where "Our bread of life" was born. Many stables were built into caves in this area. The site of Jesus' birth was likely a cave. The shepherds will come from the hills of Judah to see Jesus here.

## TOWNS ALONG EXPRESS ROUTE TO BETHLEHEM

The Via Maris was one of the two most important arteries going North and South. It was also called the "Way of the Sea". Mary and Joseph would first go from Nazareth to Caesarea, then to Joppa, Lydda and then over to Jerusalem. The towns on their route:

Dor ( Dora ) : A town of Canaanites, seven plus miles north of Caesarea.

Caesarea :   Herod built and named this after his friend, Caesar Augustus. An important town on the Mediterranean.

Joppa : Where Peter raised Tabitha (Dorcus)  from the dead.   It was the Mediterranean seaport  of ancient Israel.

Lydda: Where you'll see olive branches tied to the sides of donkeys going to market.   Peter visited it and cured a man there, resulting in a large increase of followers.

Jerusalem : Capital of Judah, of Judea, of Palestine and of Jews worldwide. When Jesus was forty days old, he was taken there to the Temple.

Bethlehem: As a village it existed as early as the time of Jacob.  Birth place of David and Jesus. Residence of Boaz, Ruth and Jesse.  It was five miles south of Jerusalem along the main highway to Hebron and Egypt.

## BELOW BETHLEHEM TO ELIZABETH'S HOME

Town in the hills of Judea: When Mary went to visit Elizabeth, she went south of Bethlehem  to Hebron. It was difficult and dangerous mountainous terrain.

## ROUTE THE WISE MEN MAY HAVE TAKEN

The Wise Men probably came to Palestine from the route which carried traffic from the eastern desert. The King's Highway came through cities east of the Sea of Galilee and east of the Dead Sea. From the King's Highway branch roads led to the country west of the Jordan to Jericho with additional branches going to Judaea and Samaria. It has not been proven where they came from, but signs seem to point to the banks of the Tigris and Euphrates where astronomy was cultivated and where the old Zen religion had been established by the Persians. Magi is a Persian word. The word magician comes from Magi.

A song may have started the myth of the three kings. Legend has them representing the three races of man. Each was given a name and brought a symbolic gift. Balthasar, a bearded black man, King of Ethiopia, carried frankincense a symbol of purification for a high priest. Melchior, an old man and King of Arabia ( maybe a Hindu) brought a casket of gold, a symbol implying the newborn was King of Kings. Gaspar, the young light-skinned King ( possibly Greek), carried myrrh, a holy ointment, symbol of a great physician, sorrow and death. Pellets of frankincense were found in the tomb of King Tutankhamen. It was exported by sea from Dhofar, or overland by camel through Medina to Petra, Damascus and other distribution points. Frankincense came into Judah by camel caravan. It brought prosperity to Southern Arabia. Therefore, one of the Wise Men was thought to be from Arabia. Isaiah 60: 6-9 says they will be from Midian, Ephah and Sheba (A wealthy land in Southern Arabia.). Look at a map to imagine the Wise Men's long slow journey across the desert following a star. On this day, let us take time to discover what star we are following. Is it Jesus?

**ROUTE TO EGYPT**

When Mary and Joseph fled to Egypt, they probably went from Jerusalem to Gaza. Then took the Via Maris south from the Gaza Strip across the
Sinai Desert toward Egypt. The Gaza Strip is a band of territory about thirty
one miles long and four miles wide. It stretches along the Mediterranean
coast from Gaza to Egypt which occupies the NE portion of Africa. On the
main road between Mesopotamia and Egypt, it is the edge of the desert junc-
tion of a trade route from Southern Arabia.

**For each one of us, there is a desert to travel**, a story to discover, and
a being within ourselves to bring to life while looking for and following Jesus.

**Route the Wise Men may have taken:**

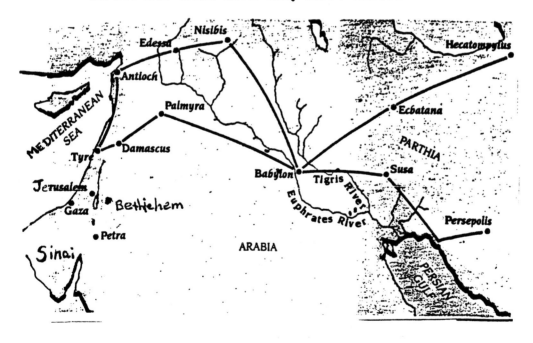

**See page 47 for larger map showing route Mary and Joseph's route.**

# CHAPTER 9

## PROPHECIES IN THE CHRISTMAS STORY
### Proof Jesus is the Messiah

When the prophets of the Old Testament foretold things to come, they were not predicting the future. The future was dependent on the present. It was an inevitable consequence of an existing situation. All the great prophets made it clear, they spoke for God. Injustice and falsehood brought punishment, for they were offenses against the law. The prophets foretell or predict only a future which is inescapable of existing conditions. They believed they were called by God to deliver God's messages

## PROPHETIC FROM OLD TESTAMENT

**Be from the Seed of Abraham-** Genesis   12: 3
And I will bless them that bless thee, and curse him that curseth thee:  and in thee shall all families of the earth be blessed.

**Be from the Seed of Isaac -**Genesis   17:19
And God said, Sarah thy wife shall bear thee a son indeed; and thou shalt call his name Isaac; and I will establish my covenant with him for an everlasting covenant, and with this seed after him.

**From the Seed of Jacob-**Numbers   24:17
I shall see him, but not now:  I shall behold him, but not nigh: there shall come a Star out of Jacob, and a Scepter shall rise out of Israel, and shall smite the corners of Moab, and destroy all the children of Sheth.

**Be from the Tribe of Judah**-Genesis 49:10

The scepter shall not depart from Judah; nor a lawgiver from between his feet, until Shiloh come; and unto him shall the gathering of the people be.

**Heir to the Throne of David**-Isaiah 9:6-7

Of the increase of his government and peace there shall be no end, upon the throne of David, and upon his kingdom, to order it, and to establish it with judgment and with justice from henceforth even for ever.  The zeal of the Lord of hosts will perform this.

**Have an Eternal Throne**-Daniel 2:44

In all the days  of these kings shall the God of heaven set up a kingdom, which shall never be destroyed: and the kingdom (the sovereignty) shall not be left to other people, but it shall break in pieces and consume all these kingdoms, and it shall stand forever.

**Be called Immanuel**-Isaiah 7:14

Therefore the Lord himself shall give you a sign; Behold, a virgin shall conceive and bear a son, and shall call his name Immanuel.

**Have a Forerunner**-Malachi 3:1

Behold I will send my messenger, and he shall prepare the way before me: and the Lord, whom ye seek, shall suddenly come to his temple, even the messenger of the covenant, : behold, he shall come, saith the Lord of hosts.

**Be born of Woman**-Genesis 3:15

And I will put enmity between thee and the woman, and between thy seed and her seed; it shall bruise thy head and thou shalt bruise his heel.

**Be Born of a Virgin-Isaiah 7: 14**

Therefore the Lord himself shall give you a sign; Behold, a virgin shall conceive, and bear a son, and shall call his name Immanuel.

**Be Born in Bethlehem-Micah 5:2**

But thou, Bethlehem Ephrathah, though thou be little among the thousands of Judah, yet out of thee shall he come forth unto me that is to be ruler in Israel; whose goings forth have been from of old, from everlasting.

**Be Worshipped by Wise Men-Isaiah 60: 3, 6, 9**

And the Gentiles shall come to thy light, and kings to the brightness of thy rising. The multitude of camels shall cover thee, the dromedaries of Midian and Ephah, all they from Sheba shall come: they shall bring gold and incense. They shall shew forth the praises of the Lord. Surely the isles shall wait for me, and the ships of Tarshish first, to bring thy sons from far, their silver and their gold with them, unto the name of the Lord thy God, and to the Holy One of Israel, because he hath glorified thee.

**Come out of Egypt-Hosea 11:14**

When Israel was a child, then I loved him and called my son out of Egypt.

**Suffer a Massacre of Infants-Jeremiah 31:15**

Thus saith the Lord: A voice was heard in Ramah, lamentation, and bitter weeping, Rachel weeping for her children refused to be comforted for her children, because they were not.

# FULFILLED IN THE NEW TESTAMENT

**Be from the Seed of Abraham**-Matthew 1 :1

The book of the generation of Jesus Christ, the son of David, the son of Abraham.

**Be from the Seed of Isaac**-Luke 3:34

Which was the son of Jacob, was the son of Isaac, which was the son of Abraham, which was the son of Nahor.

**From the Seed of Jacob**-Matthew 1:2

Abraham begat Isaac; and Isaac begat Jacob; and Jacob begat Judas and his brethren.

**Be from the Tribe of Judah**-Luke 3:33

Which was the son of Amminadab, which was the son of Ram, which was the son of Hezron, which was the son of Pharez, which was the son of Judah.

**Heir to the Throne of David**-Luke 1:32-33

He shall be great, and shall be called the Son of the Highest; and the Lord God shall give unto him the throne of his father David: And he shall reign over the house of Jacob forever; and of his kingdom there shall be no end.

**Have an Eternal Throne**-Luke 1:33

And he shall reign over the house of Jacob forever: and of his Kingdom there shall be no end.

**Be called Immanuel**-Matthew 1:23

Behold, a virgin shall be with child and shall bring forth a son, and they shall call his name Immanuel, which being interpreted is, God with us.

**Have a Forerunner**-Luke 7: 24, 27

And when the messengers of John were departed, he began to speak unto the people concerning John. What went ye out into the wilderness for to see? A reed shaken with the wind? This is he, of who it is written, Behold, I send my messenger before thy face, which shall prepare the way before thee.

**Be born of Woman**-Galatians 4:4

But when the fullness of the time was come, God sent forth his son, made of woman, made under the law.

**Be Born of a Virgin**-Luke 1:26, 27, 30, 31

And in the sixth month the angel Gabriel was sent from God unto a city of Galilee, named Nazareth. To a virgin espoused to a man whose name was Joseph, of the house of David; and the virgin's name was Mary. And the angel said unto her, Fear not, Mary: for thou has found favor with God. And behold, thou shalt conceive in the womb, and bring forth a son, and shalt call his name Jesus.

**Be Born in Bethlehem**-Luke 2:4

Joseph went up from Galilee, out of the city of Nazareth, into Judah, unto the city of David,which is called Bethlehem, because he was of the house and lineage of David. To be taxed with Mary his espoused wife, being great with child. And

she brought forth her first born son, and wrapped him in swaddling clothes, and laid him in a manger; because there was no room for them in the inn.

**Be Worshipped by Wise Men-Matthew 2:11**

And when they had come into the house, they saw the young child with Mary his mother, and fell down, and worshipped him: and when they had opened their treasures, they presented unto him gifts; gold, frankincense, and myrrh.

**Come out of Egypt-Matthew 2:14-15**

When he arose, he took the young child and his mother by night, and departed into Egypt. And was there until the death of Herod. That it might be fulfilled which was spoken by the Lord through the prophet saying, "Out of Egypt have I called my son."

**Suffer a Massacre of Infants-Matthew 2:16-18**

Then Herod, when he saw that he was mocked of the Wise Men, was exceeding angry, and sent forth, and slew all the children that were in Bethlehem, and in all the coasts thereof, from two years old and under, according to the time which he had diligently inquired of the Wise Men. Then was fulfilled that which was spoken by Jeremiah the prophet, saying, In Ramah was there a voice heard, lamentation , and weeping, and great mourning, Rachel weeping for her children, and would not be comforted because they are not.

**These prophecies clearly show us Jesus was the long awaited Messiah. These fourteen prophecies are all fulfilled in the Christmas story. More prophecies are fulfilled in Jesus' later life.** Here was the "virgin" of Isaiah's prophecy. Jesus was human as Isaiah had prophesied and yet divine because the Holy Spirit came upon Mary. Deity and humanity together for our redemption. Even the birth in Bethlehem was accomplished by God's providence through Caesar Augustus.

## Genealogy of Jesus

There are two genealogies of Jesus. Matthew and Luke have some different names on the family tree. The lines run parallel from Abraham to David, but then Matthew traces to Jesus by way of Solomon the son of David through Joseph. This is the royal line. Luke's genealogy traces Jesus by way of Nathan the son of David. This is the legal line. These two genealogies represent the lines of two brothers and their offspring who are cousins. Matthew shows the line of Joseph. Matthew and Luke differ in the names on the family tree.

Nathan was the older brother of Solomon but the younger brother took the throne. Nathan's line went through the years and ultimately produced the Virgin Mary. Solomon's line produced Joseph. Matthew does not say Joseph begat Jesus but that he was the husband of Mary, of whom was born Jesus. Matthew says Jacob was the father of Joseph. The greatest proof of all lies in the names in Matthew's account of **Jechonias,** who was accursed of God who took the throne away from him. It is the name which furnishes the reason for the inclusion of the genealogy of Jesus' step father, for it proves Joseph could not have been the father of Jesus, for if he had been, Jesus could not have been the Messiah. The use of that name is conclusive evidence Jesus is the son of Mary and not the son of Joseph. Jeremiah 22:30 says "write ye this man childless, a man that shall not prosper in his days; for no man of his seed shall prosper, sitting upon the throne of David and ruling any more in Judah." Solomon's line is the royal line and makes Jesus born of the royal line but not of the seed of Joseph.

Luke's genealogy is of Virgin Mary. Luke says "Jesus was the son, it was thought, of Joseph, the son of Heli" (Luke 3:23). Testifying to the virgin birth, he was thought to be the father but in point of fact was not. A son of Heli from the line of Nathan could be contested by the royal line.

Luke uses a word for son that includes what we call son-in-law. The dilemma is solved in a simple way. The line that had no curse on it produced Heli and his daughter, the Virgin Mary and her son Jesus Christ. He is eligible therefore by the line of Nathan and exhausts that line. The line which had a curse on it produced Joseph, who exhausts the line of Solomon. Now Joseph who, by legal adoption, has a royal heir yet not by his seed. A curse on one line and the lack of reigning royalty in the other makes the title free.

When God the Holy Spirit begat the Lord Jesus in the womb of the Virgin without any use of a human father, the child who was born was the seed of David according to the flesh. When Joseph married Mary and took the unborn child under his protecting care, giving Him the title which had come down to him through his ancestor Solomon, the Lord Jesus became the legal Messiah, the royal Messiah, the uncursed Messiah, the only possible Messiah. The lines are exhausted. No man professing to fulfill the conditions can come into this world. He would be a liar. This is truly a lesson in patience in waiting for the second coming of Christ. The people in the Old Testament waited a long time. People kept the genealogies straight because they wanted to know who might reign upon the throne. The final value is the Scripture. Second Timothy 3:16 which says, "All scripture is given to us by inspiration from God and useful to teach us."

# CHAPTER 10

## THE MEANING OF ADVENT

### Jesus Is Coming

Advent is the beginning of the Christian Year, just as New Year's Day is the beginning of the secular year. Advent means coming. The days before Christmas should give us a yearning for peace and hope. We should use Advent as a way of preparing for the royal splendor of Jesus' Second Coming. To prepare for the baby in the manger, the earthly Jesus, two resources are a Nativity set and the Advent wreath.

**A Nativity set:**

Unpack your Nativity set with this prayer from St. Andrew' Episcopal Church in Grand Rapids, Michigan. :

It is time, Lord. Time to take the holy drama from this cardboard box and set it beneath the tree. As I blow away the dust, may this little Creche come to life in our home and bestow its secret blessings.

Bless this wooden stable, Lord. This lowly abode of cows and donkeys. May it keep me humble this Christmas.

Bless this tiny star beaming at the top. May it light my eyes with the wonder and remind me "God is light."

Bless the little angel. May her song flow through our home and fill it with smiles.

Bless this caring shepherd and the small lamb cradled in his arms. May it whisper of Your caring embrace on my life.

Bless these Wise Men bearing splendid gifts. May they inspire me to lay my shining best at Your feet.

Bless this Virgin Mother. May she teach me patience as I tend to my little ones.

Bless this earthly father, Joseph, in his simple robe. May he remind me of all You have entrusted to my care.

Bless this Baby nestled in the hay. May the love He brought to earth that Bethlehem night so fill my heart with compassion and warmth that it becomes a Christmas gift to those around me.

The Creche is here, Lord and we are holy participants in Your miracle night.


**Advent wreath with four candles:**

Advent wreaths are used in the home and churches. The wreath symbolizes God has no beginning and no end. God is the Alpha and the Omega. Alpha is the first letter in the Greek alphabet and Omega is the last letter. The wreath has four candles representing the four weeks in Advent. On the first Sunday in Advent, the first candle is lit in expectation of the coming of Jesus. Each successive Sunday, one more candle shines building excitement as the Christmas story is read from the Gospels and songs sung to prepare hearts for the coming of the Christ child.

Instead of buying an expensive Advent holder, a family can circle four candlesticks with fresh evergreens. With little children it is safer to use artificial greens. Usually, the first candle is lit the first week by the youngest child. The second week the oldest child lights two. Three candles are lit by the mother the third week. The fourth week dad lights all the candles as everyone sings, "Advent tells us Christ is near, Christmas tells us Christ is here." What Advent is all about, in a way, is more difficult than Christmas. It's easier to focus on what happened in the little town of Bethlehem, then what is still to come.

**Meanings of the colors of the candles**

Some people ( like Lutherans) use blue candles to represent hope of the Second Coming. Catholics and Episcopalians use purple candles to denote Advent, like Lent, is a time for repentance and penitence. It is a time to improve ourselves for the coming of Christ. This means Christmas songs and parties have to wait until after Advent. Instead, songs like "Come the Long Expected Jesus," "The King Shall Come," "O Come, Oh Come Emmanuel," "Lo He Comes with Clouds Descending," "Prepare the Royal Highway," and "Savior of the Nations Come," are sung.

In the Roman (Catholic) rite, Advent begins looking forward to the Second Coming. It continues with the picture of important signs which will precede the arrival of Christ to judge the world. On the third Sunday, the candle is pink. The purple vestments and altar hangings are exchanged for rose-colored ones to represent joy since the Incarnation is near.

**Names of the Advent Candles:**

Different churches have various names for the four candles. Examples are:
1) A United Methodist church names the first candle **"Hope."** These words are said as the candle is lit: " We light this candle to proclaim the coming of the light of God into our darkness. With the coming of light (Jesus) there is hope. The second candle **"Love"** is lit with these words: "We light this candle as a symbol of our love. May the love sent from God give us the time for caring, sharing, and rejoicing in His love." The third candle" **Joy** " with these words: "We light this candle as a symbol of joy. May our faces radiate the joy of His coming so that everyone we meet will know Him and the gift of life He bring

The fourth candle " **Peace** " with these words: "We light this candle as a symbol of peace. May this light bring strength and hope to all of us and make us ready for your coming."

2) A Reformed Church calls the first candle " **Anticipation**"; the second "**Preparation**"; the third one, "**Proclamation** " and the fourth, "**Revelation.**

3) A Bible Church names the four candles **Mary, Joseph, Shepherds and Wise Men.** On each of the four Sundays they discuss the importance of one of these names.

**Our Advent Candle:**

Our antique ceramic Advent Wreath has a painting on each of the four sides. The paintings depict the first candle as "**Prophecy,**" honoring the prophets who foretold of the Messiah's birth; the second as " **Bethlehem,**" honoring Jesus' place of birth; the third one as the " **Shepherds,**" honoring the first visitors; and the fourth one as the" **angel,**" honoring the six times angels are in the Christmas story. See photo on page 123.

**Advent Readings:**

The Second Coming is the final deliverance which God is preparing. Sacred events don't function as they are suppose to unless they are treated as sacred. These are the sacred gospel readings read in the Catholic, Episcopal and Lutheran churches during the four weeks of Advent:

**First** Sunday in Advent: "Then shall they see the Son of Man coming in a cloud with power and great glory" (Luke 2: 27). This reading prepares many for the Second Coming.

**Second** Sunday in Advent: "Art Thou He that shall come, or are we to look for another?" (Matthew 11: 3) John sent his disciples to ask Jesus if He is the Messiah. In answering, the Gospel focuses upon the Advent theme of preparing for the coming ministry of Jesus. He is the Messiah because He fulfills the signs which the prophet Isaiah predicted would accompany His coming. John is Jesus' faithful forerunner, a prophet and the expected messenger sent to prepare the way of the Messiah.

**Third** Sunday in Advent: "I baptize you with water but He shall baptize you with the Holy Spirit." This Sunday is preparing us for the Incarnation which completes the revelation of God to man which started in the Jewish Scriptures. The Gospel for this Sunday is concerned with the real nature of Christ. We look at Jesus with the eyes of John the Baptist. John explains he is the voice sent from God to prepare the way for the Messiah who will baptize men with the Holy Spirit. The Gospel puts John the Baptist and Jesus in the context of Jewish prophecy. John is looking for the coming of Our Lord and the Old Testament prepares the way for the Messiah.

**Fourth** Sunday in Advent "And he came into all the country about Jordan, preaching and baptizing for the forgiveness of sins." Luke 3: 3 The Gospel tells of John the Baptist fulfilling Isaiah's prophecy. It points out Christ is indeed the One of whom the prophets foretold.

**Advent reflections:**

In Advent there is revitalization and a chance to reorder our lives. Christmas as a religious experience should refresh us and give us time to reflect.

Take time to find books in the Public Library with poems honoring Jesus, such as " Voices In The Mist"  By Alfred Lord Tennyson  or read the following:

**'Take a Moment in Advent"        Author  unknown**

In this season of Advent
make room for strangers and friends
Then you'll know you made room for Jesus
When Xmas comes to an end.

It only takes a moment
to do a thoughtful thing.
Just think of all the happiness
our thoughtful acts might bring.

Why, it only takes a moment
to pick up the telephone
And say hello to someone
who is sitting home alone.

And it only takes a moment
when someone is feeling blue,
To send a little Xmas note
with a loving line or two.

It only takes a moment
to extend a helping hand
Or give someone assurance
that we really understand

In this season of Advent
make room for strangers and friends
Then you'll know you made room for Jesus
When Xmas comes to an end.


**" An Advent or Christmas Letter"**  Author  unknown
 (A nice note to send to those you love.)


I have a list of folks I love, all written in a book,
And every year at Christmas time, I go and take a look.
And that is when I realize that these names are a part,
Not of the book they're written in, but of my very heart.

Each name stands for one who has crossed my path sometime,
And in that meeting I've become the "Rhythm of the Rhyme"
And while it sounds fantastic for me to make this claim,
I really feel I am composed of each remembered name

And while you may not be aware of any special link,
Just meeting you shaped my life more than you think.
For once I've met somebody, the years can not erase,
The memory of a pleasant work or a friendly face.

So never think my Christmas cards are just a mere routine

Of names, upon a Christmas list, forgotten in between.

For when I send a Christmas card that is addressed to you,

It's because you're on that list of folks indebted to.


For I am but a total of the many folks I've met,

And you happen to be one of those I prefer not to forget;

And whether I have known you many years or few,

In some ways you have had a part in shaping things I do.


And every year when Christmas comes, I realize anew

The nicest gift life can give is meeting folks like you.

May we all remember God's greatest gift, Jesus, His Son

That was born in a manger, for all of us, each and every one.


The real joy of Christmas is having Jesus in our hearts

The real hope is what the Second Coming imparts

It means life eternal was given to us by the Babe in the stable.

And after death, we'll be together, by Jesus we are able.


**An Advent Project:**

Who can forget the excitement of waiting for Christmas. An Advent Calendar with cookies or felt figures tucked inside can help the children count the days. Cut a large piece of felt on which to sew four rows of seven pockets. In each pocket place a wrapped cookie and a verse from the Christmas story. Felt figures or animals can represent those on the verse. See picture in Chapter 6.

Start three days before December. Numbers put on the pockets to help small children know how many days are left. They should be in count-down fashion starting with number 28. Each day the anticipation builds towards the real meaning of Christmas by having the children remove the figure from the pocket for that day and place it on the upper part of the felt. The children then read the verse and decide if the figures from yesterday are still needed or should be put back in their pocket. A cookie is a reward for the right reply.

**Advent Activities:**

1. An old German Lutheran custom is to add a paper star to the wreath each Sunday. These stars have an Old Testament verse on one side and a New Testament verse on the other. These are to be memorized and discussed during the week. Prophecies in Chapter Nine can be used for this project.

2. Every Sunday give or make a new Nativity figure for each of your children. Do projects from a chapter which fits the age group of your children.

3. When you mail your Christmas cards. Remember, "Jesus is the reason for the season," by sending religious cards and postage stamps which honor Jesus.

4. If you're late getting out your cards, send cards with Wise Men on them. You can explain you didn't send your cards earlier before because the Wise Men shouldn't arrive until January 6th.

**Gifts to buy that can have eternal value:**

Buy Christian books as gifts. To order this book use form on the back page. Excellent gift ideas, which could have eternal value are in "The Samaritan's Purse Christmas Catalog." It offers a number of items for those friends, who have everything. The gift is given in their name.

Write for the Samaritan's Purse Christmas Catalog at P.O. Box 3000, Boone, N.C. 28607 or call 1-800-353-5957.

Among the gifts are:

1) A supply of 20 hens and a rooster that will furnish a family with food to eat or sell, for a cost of $6. per chicken. " The poor will eat and be satisfied; they who seek the Lord will praise him "( Psalm 22:26).

2) A seed kit that can give a family a new start and bring opportunities to sow the good seed of God's word, for the cost of $5. " As the soil makes the sprouts come up and a garden causes seed to grow, so the Lord will make righteousness and praise spring up from all nations"( Isaiah 61:11).

3) A gift of $7 can furnish a homeless child with a hot meal and shelter every night for a week. " A father to the fatherless, a defender of widows, is God in his holy dwelling" (Psalm 68: 5).


**Our family's Advent preparation:**

Welcome, come on in ! We want to share our Advent tradition with you. On the first Sunday in Advent, we light the first candle on our Advent Wreath. We then remind the children that on each Sunday in Advent, they will receive one of the nativity figures they ordered last Epiphany. It was easy at first to fulfill their request of Mary, Joseph, Jesus, shepherds, lambs and Wise Men. However, as years went on, they listened more intently to the Christmas Story and wanted additional figures of the populace. They requested King Herod, Simeon, Zachariah and Anna. Then they wanted a house for Mary and one for Elizabeth, pots, pans and furniture. We had three children. Therefore, three children times four Sundays in Advent meant twelve new items every year. That is how we acquired over six hundred pieces. The rules were simple. If they could find the person in the story, they could order that individual. If something was not mentioned in the story, like King Herod's palace and Hanukkah candles, they had to do research to find out how the item fit into the real story. We prepare for the Christmas story, each year knowing we will learn something new. We have for over forty years. Even when we read the Old Testament, it jumps out at us and says, " I'm part of the Christmas story, too." It really makes the story come alive.

## "Let every heart prepare Him Room"

Please join us in a walk through our home to see how we have made room for Jesus. Our motto is, "Let every room and heart prepare for Him." It is a joy every year to have hundreds of people stop by to see and hear the story. We begin our witness in the living room by explaining how many of the prophecies in the Old Testament came true in the Christmas story. This is where we have our oldest and largest set, about six hundred figures. They are five inches tall. Many are Fontanini, an import from Italy. The room is a delight to children since they are allowed to touch and move the figures, thus making the Bible come alive to them. Yes, we do have accidents. A villager had her foot broken off. Ken is great with glue. The woman now has a brace-let where her foot was reattached. Our granddaughter marveled the lady was healed.

The room is set up in a geographical pattern to suggest the map of Palestine. Nazareth, in the North, is the home of Mary and her parents and Joseph's home and carpenter shop. Judea, in the South, has Elizabeth's home, and the hills for the shepherds, Jerusalem with King Herod's palace, the Jewish Temple, and Bethlehem with the inn, stable and census taker. In the East are Magi studying the stars before they start on their journey. In the Northeast, we place Caesar Augustus, who is visiting in Syria where Quirinius is Governor.

Hundreds of angels are hanging from the door jams or set on the top of our tallest pieces of furniture. In our front hall we display the Christmas cards we receive which honor Jesus. Of course, we try to witness by sending only religious postage stamps and cards.

In our dining room, we display the Advent Wreath, the Jesse Tree and serve the birthday cake for Jesus. We serve cookies made in the shape of symbols of Christ's birth, along with tea served in angel cups. On Epiphany, we use a camel teapot with matching cups and serve a Wise Man-shaped cake. A gingerbread stable, with figures made of bread dough, is in the kitchen.

The music room has many music boxes. Here we explain how and why carols were written. We have a horn to represent the horn of salvation and a bell collection to help ring in Christ's birth. The "Jesus of the world" room has Nativity sets from many lands.

One bedroom has a great visual aid showing a village with the stable as a carved out cave below the inn. This is more in keeping with the type of stable where Jesus was born. In another bedroom, the Tiffany Nativity set is on display showing the special gifts to Jesus from the Wise Men. There is pure myrrh and frankincense as it comes off trees, oil of myrrh for people to apply on their wrist and frankincense to burn for fragrance.

The Angel bedroom has shepherds standing beneath an angel tree. It symbolizes the awesomeness of having the heavenly host being above the shepherds' heads. On the bed are angels for the children to cuddle. Around the room are male and female angels of different ethnic background doing different jobs and some very strong in appearance who remind us of the angels in the Bible. In our walk-in closet, we display many pins and a variety of sweat shirts illustrating the Advent and Christmas Season. Plus we have a special statue of Joseph, the foster parent, holding Jesus.

On the walls throughout our home are cross-stitched nativity scenes made by my husband. In the family room, there is a Nativity picture on a tapestry, one on a slate and one etched on glass plus our special set that was made by our children thirty- five years ago. Our son, David, started it in the third grade when he made a beautiful Saint Luke out of cardboard and linen. Initially, we used it to top off our Christmas tree. Later, our children made a complete Nativity set matching the gospel writer.

The grandchildren's play room has many Creches: A tiny one in the Barbie's doll house; a felt one which can be moved each day; an antique child's Creche; and an unbreakable pewter one which is a magnet to little hands. Beside the book, called " The Best Christmas Pageant Ever," is a set with the little children dressed for the pageant and Jesus in a little red wagon. We have a felt Advent calendar with all the characters and many puppets to help tell the story. We have VCR tapes as well as Nintendo games which convey the Good News of Jesus and His birth.

Ken's work room turns into the carpenter's shop where children may use the tools of Jesus' day. Here we have a hand-carved Nativity set and one cut out of wood on a jig saw, plus a wooden nativity puzzle.
In our front coat closet, we have a gold set from France. In the back door coat closet, we have a " Precious Moments " set with a carved out cave.

The master bathroom has a paper mache set with Jesus wrapped in swaddling bands. The guest bath has a needlepoint set with palm trees, made by our eighty-year old friend Catherine Priebe. The downstairs bathroom has a Native American set with hands forming the stable. Also downstairs, in the laundry room, we have a Nativity set made of clothes pins and one made of washable material. On the sewing machine, is a thimble with the Holy Family painted on it and hanging over it is a nativity quilt.

Our hearts can't keep all the joy about the birth of Jesus on the inside, so we let it flow out into the world. The First Sunday of Advent we put a life-size Mary and Angel outside in the front yard. The next day the angel is with Joseph. Then the Holy couple is placed at the edge of our property to begin the journey to the empty stable. The figures of Mary and Joseph are moved each day to show the progress in the journey. Our neighbors told us they thought we couldn't make up our mind until it occurred on them we were telling a story! In the back yard, the tree-house has its own Nativity set and another one is near the hill where the neighborhood children slide down. On our porch are bird houses with signs that say "No room at this inn," plus our bird feeder is shaped like a stable. There might not be room in the inn but the birds flock to the stable to share a meal with the mini Holy Family. Hope this tour gave you some ideas on how to prepare for Jesus. May you enjoy Advent and Christmas as much as our family does.

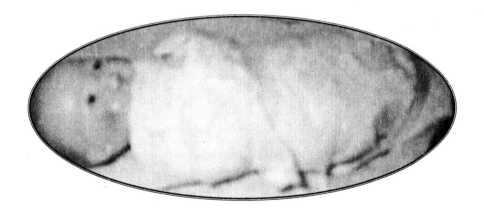

**A doll wrapped in swaddling bands.**

## CHAPTER 11
### CHRISTMAS EVE
**"Twas The Night Before Christ Birth"**

**"Twas The Night Before Christ Birth"     Author   Unknown**

'Twas the night before Christ's birth
when all through the town
Many people were hustling and bustling around,
For the night time had fallen and inn lights grew dim
In  the  city of David that's called Bethlehem.

Many others were sleeping, all cozy in beds
With soft pillows and blankets pulled up to their heads
For the trip through the desert had been hard and long,
A most difficult journey for even the strong.

But just entering the city so tired and worn
Came sweet Mary, with  Jesus  about to be born.
On the back of a donkey all night she did ride
With dear Joseph, her husband, right there by her side.

From one inn to another, they searched in despair!
But the rooms were all filled,  not a corner to spare!
An old stable where horses and cows and the like
Was the only place left to give rest for the night.

In the meantime, while shepherds were tending their sheep
In a sheep fold nearby; they were startled from sleep
For from heaven above came a glorious surprise!
Many angels appeared right in front of their eyes!

Now there wasn't a question...there wasn't a doubt!
They could hear all those angels that shone 'round about
Saying "Glory to God and goodwill to all men!
In a manger you'll find mankind's Savior from sin."

So they rushed to the city in search of this babe
That the angels had said in a manger was laid.
And, you know when they found him they heard angels sing:
For their hearts came aglow as they gazed on their King.

In the East there were wise men who came from afar
As they saw in the heavens the long promised star
That would show them the place of the King of the Jews;
For they wanted to see Him and spread the good news!

Now the Star was their guide until Jesus they found.
And they worshipped and loved Him and bowed to the ground.
Then they gave Him some Frankincense, myrrh and some gold
And arose to depart to their countries of old.

Now remember the Shepherds that heard angels sing
As you think of your Savior, your Lord and your King.

And remember the men who were wise from the start
Now ask JESUS the CHRIST to come live in your heart!

Make it a tradition to read a poem from this chapter on Christmas Eve.

After the poem play the Christmas Eve " Knock, knock" game explained in
Chapter 5.    The Christmas story needs to be told afresh before putting Mary
and Joseph in the stable.   Kiss the kids good-night. Tell them if Jesus is in the
stable in the morning they may wake you up to open one present.    They must
wait awhile longer to open more gifts.    This is a safe-guard in case they wake
up at 5 a.m.    Before you go to bed put Jesus in the manger.    If you forget, and
the children wake up early send them back to bed. Then quickly put Jesus in
the manger.    Then when they look again, He'll be there.

**"Twas The Night Before Jesus Came "    Author Unknown**
( For older children to read )

'Twas the Night before Jesus came and all through the house
Not a creature was praying, not one in the house.
Their Bibles were lain on the shelf without care,
In hopes that Jesus would not come there.

The children were dressing to crawl into bed
Not once even kneeling or bowing a head.
And Mom in her rocker with baby in her lap
was watching the Late show while I took a nap.

When out of the sky there arose such a clatter,

I sprang to my feet to see what was the matter.

Away to the window I flew like a flash

Tore open the shutters and threw up the sash!

When what to my wondering eyes should appear,

But angels proclaiming that Jesus was here.

With a light like the sun sending forth a bright ray,

I knew in a moment this must be the day!

The light of His face made me cover my head

It was Jesus! Returning just like He had said.

And though I possessed worldly wisdom and wealth,

I cried when I saw Him in spite of myself.

In the Book of Life, He held in His hand,

Was written the name of every saved man.

He spoke not a word as He searched for my name,

When He said, "It's not here" my head hung in shame.

The people whose name had been written with love,

He gathered to take to His father above.

With those who were ready, He rose without a sound

While all the rest were left standing around.

I heard him exclaim as He rose from sight,

You should have believed because the Bible was right!

## THE LEGEND OF THE FIRST CRECHE

More than seven hundred years ago, in Greccio, Italy, there lived a wood carver named Luigi. He had been a devout man until his daughter had become blind. Since then he hadn't gone to church. In mid-December in 1207 a mule train brought a piece of ivory, large as a man's thigh. Luigi knew he wanted it . He would carve a doll- a bambino- for his daughter. In three days he had an image of a new born baby chiseled from the ivory. He asked his wife to make clothes for it. On Christmas Eve, Luigi's wife begged him to go to church but he would not. When Luigi wasn't looking his wife took the bambino to church to be blessed. When Luigi found it missing he rushed to the church to get it back. When he arrived, men were bringing animals to the church. The friar said, "Come in and see my 'praesepe'--my manger scene. Luigi said he wasn't a believer any more but the friar invited him in anyway.

Inside the dimly lit church, he could see his wife kneeling by the manger. All the people gazed at Luigi's handiwork. They said they saw the bambino move but it was just the candlelight. Luigi was so moved he gave the church the bambino. He went home and stayed up all night and carved his daughter a whole 'praesepe' for her to touch........animals, manger and baby Jesus.

By Megan Hawley
Age 6

The best thing about the season is the nativityset.

Our granddaughter went to Oak Park School in Traverse City. When Megan
(Hawley) was in first grade, her teacher, Renee Sanders gave the class an
assignment, to draw and write about the best thing, in regard to the season.
We were elated Megan picked the Nativity set over Santa and his gifts.

## CHAPTER 12
## CHRISTMAS DAY
## The Twelve Days of Christmas

Familiarity breeds a boring and colorless Christmas story unless we can make it real. Start Christmas day looking for Jesus in the manger. No Jesus. No gifts. A birthday party can't start without the guest of honor. Then place a candle on a birthday or coffee cake and sing 'Happy Birthday Dear Jesus.' A white candle is added to the middle of the Advent wreath or the four candles are changed to white for the purity of Jesus. Thus the Advent Wreath becomes a Christmas Wreath. Later in the day, move the angels to appear to the shepherds. Then move the shepherds to the stable to honor Jesus.

### Xmas Prayer--Author unknown

Heavenly Father:

Christmas began

with the gift of your Son

who, in turn, gave the world

the gift of His life.

Let me remember, O God,

that Christmas remains

a matter of giving--

not parties, not present,

not material wealth--

for Christmas is Christmas

when I give of myself.

## Xmas

Christmas comes from the word Cristes Maesse, an English phrase that means the Mass of Christ. The word "Xmas" started in the early Christian Church. In Greek, X is the first letter of Christ's name. It was frequently used as a holy symbol. The story of Christmas comes from the Gospels of Saint Luke and Saint Matthew in the New Testament. Many people think, the X symbol is a way of taking Christ out of Christmas, but it is a holy symbol. The word Christmas has been used since 1038. Xmas has been used since the fourteenth century. The Greek name for Christ translated into the Roman alphabet as Khritos. The first two letters in Kristos are chi and rho and can be written XP. During the reign of Constantine the Great (306-337), it is reported that, while engaged in battle, he saw in a vision, with his own eyes, a cross bearing the inscription, "conquer by this." As a result of this vision, he marked the shields of his soldiers with " Chi Rho," Christ's monogram which form the shape of the cross. He won the decisive battle.

## Christos Kyrios

When the angel said to the shepherds the child, who had been  born in Bethlehem, was "Christ the Lord" the Greek words were Christos Kyrios. The ending of both words is masculine and in the nominative case, thus making the words equivalents. If he had used Christos Kyriou the phrase would mean   " the Lord's Christ". Christ the Lord means "Christ who is Lord," which means he wasn't just an anointed one but was actually God now manifest in human form.

## Xmas   Activities

Read   " What Can I Give Him " by Christina Rossetti ; "Christ Child" by Hans

Christian Anderson;  " Christmas Carol " by Phillips Brooks;  "Christmas is Remembering " by Elsie ;Binns;and  some of the following poems and articles.

## " Rules for Christmas"    Author Unknown

Begin the day with Jesus
Kneel down to Him in prayer,
Lift up thy heart to His abode
And seek His love to share.

Open the Book of Luke
And read a portion there,
That it may hallow all thy thoughts,
And sweeten all thy care.

Go through the day with Jesus
Whatever thy work may be,
Shoveling the walk or trimming the tree,
He still is near to thee.

Lie down at night with Jesus
Who gives His children sleep,
Remember why He came to earth
And this night His birthday keep.

## "Day Dawn In The Heart"  Author  Unknown

'Tis not enough that Christ was born

Beneath the star that shone,

And brings the day of love and good,

Within a golden zone.

He must be born within the heart

Before He finds a throne,

And brings the day of love and good,

The reign of Christlike brotherhood.


## "If Jesus Came to Your House For Xmas"        Author  unknown

If Jesus came to your house to spend Christmas with you.

If he came for Christmas, I wonder what would you do?

Oh, I know you would give your nicest room to such an honored guest.

And all the food you serve to Him would be the very best.

And you would keep assuring Him you're glad to have Him there;

That serving Him in your home is joy beyond compare.

But when you saw Him coming, would you meet Him at the door,

with arms outstretched in welcome to your heavenly visitor?

Would you say come in and share our food and see our tree ?

Would you say we just baked a birthday cake to remember thee?

Or would you take down your decor before you let Him in,

and hide your Santas and put the nativity set where Santa had been

It might be interesting to note the things that you would do.

If Jesus Christ, in person, came to spend Christmas day with you

**Song to tune of Jingle Bells by Gwen Prong**

Christmas bells, Christmas bell

telling all the day

Oh what joy it is to learn of Jesus ' birth to day Yea

Good News bells, Good News bells

Angels from on high

telling of our Savior's birth while flying in the sky

Dashing to the stable leaving their lambs behind

over the fields they go with excitement on their minds

Bells on animals ring making spirits rise

oh what excitement it is to learn of Jesus' birth tonight

**"A Little Child"  Author Unknown**

| | |
|---|---|
| A little child | Yet, in that place |
| A shining star. | So crude, forlorn, |
| A stable rude, | The Hope of all |
| A door ajar. | The world was born. |

**Date of Christmas**

The Bible does not tell the exact date for Christmas.  It was celebrated first in the fourth century.  The early church had no fixed date.  It might have been fall or summer since shepherds were in the fields.  Sheep were usually kept indoors in the winter.  Some thought May or January.  Early Christians were more interested in Jesus' Second Coming than His birth date. By the third century, it was celebrated on different dates. The first time December 25th was used was in the year 336. It was celebrated on January 6th. to commemorate the birth and baptism of Jesus in some eastern churches. Choice of December 25th was partly influenced by a theory of the Roman ecclesiastica writer, Hippolytus, who concluded the crucifixion took place in AD 29 on the 25th of March and the Annunication took place on the same day, because he believed an exact number of days elapsed between the Incarnation and the death of Christ. It followed, therefore, Christ's birth was the 25th of December.

The Reformation, a religious movement of the 1500s, gave birth to Protestantism. Many Christians at that time considered Christmas pagan because it included non-religious customs. In 1620, when the Pilgrims arrived in Plymouth, Massachusetts, they eschewed all those customs with pagan origins. They protested the laxity of the Church of England refusing to recognize Christmas. In 1643, the English Parliament denounced the festivals and passed a law prohibiting any celebration and announced the only fitting way to commemorate the birth of Christ was to fast. They employed troops to patrol the streets to ensure no one cooked a lunch for Christmas in violation of the law. In 1659, a Massachusetts law fined people for celebrating December 25th. By 1660, people started to exchange gifts and use old customs again.

Due to widespread ignoring of the law, it was repealed in 1681. Lutherans, Roman Catholics, members of the Dutch Reformed and Anglican churches were largely responsible for establishing Christmas traditions again. The date we celebrate as Jesus' birth isn't as important as how we celebrate it, and the fact we give homage to "the word was made flesh and dwelt among us."

## The Holy Land - Bethlehem

It is a wonderful experience to go to the Holy Land where Jesus was born.
A church built by Helena, the mother of Constantine sets over the natural cave
said to be the stable in which the nativity took place. A silver star marks the
place where the manger was said to have been laid. The entrance is very
small for two reasons: Spiritually, it causes everyone to bow as they come
through the entrance and militarily, horses could not be ridden through it.
The riders would have to get off their horses.

## Santa Claus

Pastor Klaus is the International Pastoral Adviser for the Lutheran Hour Minis-
tries. The Rev. Ken Klaus wrote me, "As far as 'Santa' is concerned, he and I
have been linked together for a good many years (as you have already guess-
ed). I certainly encourage the idea of celebrating without him or, celebrating
with him, if he is properly understood, i.e., a bishop who sacrificed himself for
others, in the name of Jesus, a Christian who underwent torture for his Savior;
a co-author of the Nicene Creed." The Santa most people collect does not honor
the bishop. They are of the commercial variety. They are the myth that pass
es out gifts from a sleigh. Non-Christians can celebrate the spirit of Christmas
since a baby is not a problem as long as they do not have to accept the
message of Jesus as their Savior. They can counterfeit the real meaning of
Christmas by celebrating a lesser gift giver. They put Santa and his material
gifts in the inn and God's gift of redemption in the stable. Some Jewish people
display a Santa collection during Hanakkuh. They don't perceive it as celebrating Jesus' birth. God gave us baby Jesus as our gift, when God wanted to
communicate His nature to humans, God manifested as a baby. There is God's
WORD. The word is Jesus.

**Where the Christmas Story Is Told:**

Most people read the story in the gospels of Matthew and Luke. The Lord's story is in the fortieth Psalm and is repeated in Hebrews 10: 5-7 (below).

"Sacrifice and offering you did not desire,

but **a body you prepared for me;**

with burnt offerings and sin offerings

you were not pleased.

Then I said, 'Here I am--it is written

about me in the scroll---

**I have come to do your will, O God.'** "

Jesus says He came into our world and was conscious of coming for a purpose. God willed Jesus to be our savior. He came into this world and took a human body to die for our salvation. He came with the knowledge that he was the perfect one to provide salvation for mankind. The Christmas story has Jesus born in a stable but His coming never ends because He comes again through the person of the Holy Spirit. That's the reason the Christmas story never ends. In "O Little Town of Bethlehem," we sing, "Where meek souls will receive Him still, The dear Christ enters in." God's message is simple. It is reflected in a song lyric: "Christmas isn't Christmas 'til it happens in your heart; somewhere deep inside you is where Christmas really starts. So give your heart to Jesus, you'll discover when you do, that it's Christmas, really Christmas for you."

## Twelve Days of Christmas

The twelve days of Christmas begins Christmas day and ends on January 5th. From 1558 til 1829, some Christians in England were forbidden by law to practice their faith yet they wanted their children to know about it. So just as the early Christians would draw a fish in the sand to greet one another, the "Twelve Days of Christmas" became the secret code song of Christians.

## Code for " The Twelve Days of Christmas"

My True Love is God Himself

**1st Day** - A Partridge stands for Christ, who gathers his young under his wings (Matthew 23 : 37). In Luke 13:31-35, Jesus says, " I have longed to gather your children, together, as a hen gathers her chicks under her wings." Brooding gives life plus a hen is willing to die sitting on the nest protecting her chicks. The pear tree hearkens back to the tree of paradise, which Adam lost by sin and Christ promised to restore. It also reminds us of Isaiah 11:1 " There shall come forth a shoot from the stump of Jesse, and a branch shall grow out of his roots." God's first gift is Jesus.

**2nd Day** -Two turtle doves represent the sacrifice a Jewish family made at the temple upon the birth of a son. Mary and Joseph brought doves to the temple after Christ was born.

**3rd Day** - Three French hens symbolize the three gifts from the Magi to baby Jesus. Also Faith, Love and Charity realized in the birth of the Savior.

**4th Day** - Four calling birds represent the four evangelists who called others to follow Christ; also the four gospels.

**5th Day** - Five golden rings represent the five books of the Old Testament, the books of Genesis, Exodus, Leviticus, Numbers, and Deuteronomy, which Christ came to fulfill;

**6th Day** - Six geese a-laying represent the six days when humanity labors and brings forth the fruit of the land.

**7th Day** - Seven swans a-swimming represent the seven gifts of the Holy Spirit: Apostles, prophets, teachers, miracles, power to heal, speak in tongues and to help and direct others  (1 Cor. 12: 27).

**8th Day** - Eight maids a-milking represent the nourishment (milk) of the eight  beatitudes of the Christian (Matt. 5: 1-12).

1. "Blessed are those who are spiritually poor, the kingdom of heaven belongs to them.

2. Blessed are those that mourn, for they shall be comforted.

3. Blessed are the meek, for they shall inherit the earth.

4. Blessed are those that hunger and thirst for righteousness, for they shall be filled.

5. Blessed are the merciful, for they shall obtain mercy.

6. Blessed are the pure in heart, for they shall see God.

7. Blessed are the peace makers,, for they shall be called sons of God.

8. Blessed are the persecuted for righteousness sake, for theirs is the kingdom of heaven.''

**9th Day** - Nine ladies dancing recalls the joy of the nine fruits of the Holy Spirit as mentioned by Saint Paul in Galations 5: 22: Love, Joy, Peace, Patience, Kindness, Goodness, Faithfulness, Humility and Self-Control.

**10th Day** - Ten lords a-leaping represent the Ten Commandments

(1) You shall have no other gods.

(2) You shall not make any graven image. You shall not bow down to them.

(3) You shall not misuse the name of the Lord your God.

(4) Remember the Sabbath day by keeping it holy.

(5) Honor your mother and your father.

(6) You shall not murder.

(7) You shall not commit adultery.

(8) You shall not steal.

(9) You shall not give false testimony against your neighbor.

(10) You shall not covet your neighbor's house.

You shall not covet your neighbor's wife, manservant, donkey or anything that belongs to your neighbor.

**11th Day** - Eleven pipers piping refers to the eleven Apostles without Judas.

**12th Day** - Twelve drummers drumming were to remind the faithful of the twelve articles of faith in the Nicene Creed.

(1). I believe in one God, the Father Almighty, maker of heaven and earth and of all things visible and invisible.

(2.) And in one Lord Jesus Christ, the only-begotten Son of God, begotten of his Father before all worlds, God of Light, Light of light, very God of very God,

(3.) begotten, not made, being of one substance with the Father, by whom all things are made;

(4.) who for us men and for our salvation came down from heaven and was

(5.) incarnate by the Holy Ghost of the virgin Mary and was made man;

(6.) and was crucified also for us under Pontius Pilate.

(7.) He suffered and was buried.

(8.) And the third day he rose again according to the scriptures and ascended into heaven and sits at the right hand of the Father.

(9.) And He will come again with glory to judge both the living and the dead, whose kingdom will have no end.

(10.) And I believe in the Holy Spirit, the Lord and giver of life, who proceeds from the Father and the Son, who with the Father and Son together is worshipped and glorified, who spoke by the prophets.

(11.) And I believe in one holy Catholic and apostolic Church,

(12.) I acknowledge one Baptism for the remission of sin, and I look for the resurrection of the dead and the life of the world to come.


## Special days within the 12 days of Christmas

December 25th Christmastide, The Nativity of our Lord or Birthday of Christ , commonly called Christmas Day ( John 1:1 and Luke 2: 1 )

Dec. 26th St. Stephen's Day, Deacon and Martyr ( Acts 7:55)

Dec. 27th St. John's Day, Apostle and Evangelist ( John 21:19)

Dec. 28th The Holy Innocents and Martyrs ( Matthew 2:13)

Jan. 1st The Circumcision of Christ and Name day-Secular New Year's Day

Jan. 6th Epiphany or the Manifestation of Christ to the Gentiles

# CHAPTER 13
## EPIPHANY
### Wise Men's Gifts

**Epiphany** sounds like a fairy tale, with kings in exotic garments, riding on magnificent elephants, camels and horses in a large caravan. All coming to see Jesus. The towns people must have been astonished and King Herod very nervous. Even Mary and Joseph were probably in awe of them. Epiphany is the Greek word for manifestation. Manifest means to prove, to reveal and to make clear. Epiphany is celebrated January 6th. It originated in the Eastern Church. In A.D. 200, it was mentioned by Clement of Alexandria. This makes it older than Christmas. At that time, there were only three special holy days: Easter, Pentecost and Epiphany. In the East, it still is celebrated in commemoration of the Baptism of Christ as the manifestation of the Incarnation. By the fourth century its observation was a day commonly chosen for the baptism of converts. It was a commemoration of the Christ's manifestation to the Gentiles, the Wise Men. The evening preceding Epiphany is called the Twelfth Night of Christmas, since there are twelve days of Christmas.

**The Wise Men** were serious scholars from a different part of the world. They were the first representatives of the gentile world for whom Christ came. They were very distinct from the shepherds who were Jewish and had long expected a Messiah because of the prophecies in Scripture. The Magi were a priestly caste which specialized in dreams. They claimed the gift of prophecy. The song, "We Three Kings," explains the prophecy of the gifts.

"Born a King of Bethlehem, plain. Gold I bring to crown Him again,
King forever, ceasing never over us all to reign.
Frankincense to offer have I, Incense owns a Deity nigh,
Prayer and praising, all men raising, to worship Him, God on High.
Myrrh is mine, it's bitter perfume, Breathes a life of gathering gloom.
Sorrowing, sighing, bleeding, dying, Sealed in the stone-cold tomb."

It has not been determined when the Wise Men arrived. We can surmise they did not come at the time of Jesus' birth since the family was now in a house. We can perceive from the fact that Herod ordered all male babies, two and under, killed in keeping with the information the Wise Men gave him, that Jesus was now older. The Bible says when the Wise Men came they fell down and worshipped the child (not baby). They might have told Herod they had been searching only for one year and Herod added another year. Hence, to be certain the new King of the Jews would be executed. From their study of the stars, the Wise Men knew something unprecedented had happened. They expected a special star to fulfill prophecies of Balaam and Daniel (Numbers 24:17 and Daniel 7: 13-14). Astrology is disdained in the Bible. However, God used the Magi to fulfill the prophecy of old and testify Jesus came for all nations, people and beliefs. Matthew does not mention their names or their number. There could have been three, seven, twelve or even hundreds. He did not seem to believe age or race was important. The symbolism of their gifts was more important than the bearers.

**Wise Men's Gifts**

**Gold** was a precious metal in Jesus' day just as it is now. It was a gift for a

King. Jesus is our King of Kings. The presence of gold explains why the Holy Family had money for a flight to Egypt. When needed, God provided funds. Luke 2:24 reveals Jesus was born into poverty. The law required a lamb as a sacrifice on this occasion unless the woman was poor ( Lev. 12: 6to 8). Then she was allowed to offer two inexpensive turtledoves, like Mary did.

**Frankincense** was a gift for a High Priest. "God declared Jesus to be High Priest in the order of Melchizedek," in Hebrews 5:10 and 6: 20. Frankincense was valued the same as gold and jewels when the Magi brought it. It's smoke was thought to reach the heavens as no other, taking prayers with it. Resin of the frankincense tree (Boswllia Sacra), like myrrh and aloes wood, is one of a number of aromatic substances which, when burned, give off a pleasurable pungent smell. This minor characteristic was esteemed so highly in ancient cultures, almost all people of the Mediterranean and the Middle East thought it vital to their religious rituals. Some believed the fragrant white smoke from smoldering incense soothed an angry God. Harvesting it was difficult. First they would shave strips of bark from the Frankincense trunk. Tears of resin formed where the nomads made cuts in the bark. The collectors used an a putty knife like instrument , called a mingaf. Resin would ooze from these wounds and harden into crystals and then scraped off the tree. If the luban (resin) fell off the tree to the ground it would be lighter and cleaner. It would be dried naturally. This collection began in the winter, peaked in spring and ended with summer monsoons. With the decline of the Roman Empire, the demand for incense slackened, though Christians used incense at high masses. The perfumed smoke also repelled bugs and helped to relieve asthma. It was used as perfume in Song of Sol. 3: 6 but most frequently used in a religious context. Exodus 30: 34, contains the recipe for a frankincense- based incense dedicated for ritual use. Exodus 30:9 states no other incense was permitted on the altar. Exodus 30: 38 says secular use was forbidden. Lev.2:1-2,14-18 says it accompanied cereal offerings, but could not be used as a sin offering.

**Myrrh** was used for burials. It was a personification of our savior. Jesus would die for our sins. John 19: 39, says, " Nicodemus, the man who had come to Jesus at night, went with Joseph taking with him about one hundred pounds of embalming ointment made from a mixture of myrrh and aloes. Together they wrapped Jesus' body in long linen cloth saturated with the spices, as is the Jewish custom of burial." On the cross, Matthew 27:34 tells "When Jesus had tasted thereof, he would not drink." Mark 15:23 states "There they tried to give Him wine mixed with a drug called myrrh but Jesus would not drink it." Myrrh would deaden the pain. Myrrh was an oil designed for anointing the dead. It was a gift for our Savior at birth and was a holy preparation for the tomb.

The **myrrh** tree's bark is brittle and often cracks of its own accord. Gatherers have little work to do in collecting it. When hardened, the sap is dark and bitter tasting, unlike frankincense which is pale and sweet. Myrrh prefers basaltic soils to limestone. It cost five times as much as frankincense and had a wider range. It was a status symbol. Just a drop of myrrh oil could double the price of cheaper perfumes. Egyptians used myrrh to embalm royal mummies. When King Tut's tomb was opened in 1922, the air was still thick with the strong scent. Myrrh was recommended by Chinese doctors to be mixed with mother's milk and used as a cure for diaper rash. Turks claimed the same mixture was an aphrodisiac. Arab men drank myrrh and vinegar to cure baldness. Healers in India said it cured obesity and extended life. Recently in India, scientists found one species that lowered serum cholesterol levels in monkeys by thirty percent.

**To order the Wise men's gifts send for a catalog from Rafal Spice**
Company 2521 Russell, Detroit, MI 48207
Frankincense # 590800 cost $5.19 for 1/2 oz. oil
Frankincense #060904 Resin Tears cost $ 2.24 for 2 oz.
Frankincense # 060919 powdered cost $2.42 for 2 oz.
Myrrh #592000 cost $6.39 for 1/2 ounce.

**Epiphany Cake** was an ornamental cake, with two beans inside it, baked on Epiphany by people in New Orleans. Whoever drew the beans became the King and Queen of the festivities. Our tradition is to bake a different kind of cake, in keeping with the Wise Men's gifts. Just as their gifts were symbolic, we put items in our cake representing the fruit of the spirit ( Galations 5: 22.) The symbols are guides to revitalizing our sensitivity to how we reflect the fruit in our life. If we receive joy, we contemplate new ways to bring joy to others and perceive when joy is given to us. Christ manifested the fruit of the Spirit in his life. The idea is simple. Bake a cake in the shape of a Wise Man or a bundt cake which represents a crown. After the cake cools, turn it over. Place inside the cake a number of small articles symbolizing the "fruit of the spirit," wrapped individually in Saran wrap. Put about two inches apart. Turn upright and frost. Gather loved ones around the cake. Each person picks the piece they want. If the cake is shaped like a Wise Man, someone might want the hand or foot. Before eating their portion, the person finds their "fruit " and exchanges it for a card.

154

The card has this verse from Galatians 5:22 on it  plus a verse to go with the symbol : "But when the Holy Spirit controls our lives he will produce this kind of fruit in us: **love, joy, peace, patience, kindness, goodness, faithfulness, gentleness, self-control."**

The corresponding Bible verses and their symbols are listed below:

### A heart = love- 1 Corinthians 13: 4-8

"Love suffers long and is kind; love does not envy; love does not parade itself, it is not puffed up, does not behave rudely, does not seek its own, is not pro voked, thinks no evil, does not rejoice in iniquity, but rejoices in the truth; bears all things, believes all things, hopes all things, endures all things. Love never fails."

### A bell = joy  - Romans 14: 17

"For the kingdom of God is not eating and drinking, but righteous and peace and joy in the Holy Spirit."    Or Eccl. 2:26, "For God gives those who please Him wisdom, knowledge, and joy."   Or John 15:11, "These things I have spoken to you, that my joy may remain in you and your joy may be filled."

### A dove = peace   - Phil. 4: 6-7

"Don't worry about anything; instead, pray about everything; tell God your needs and don't forget to thank Him for His answers.  If you do this you will experience God's peace, which is far more wonderful than the human mind can understand.  His peace will keep your thoughts and your heart quiet and at rest as you trust in Christ Jesus."

### A cross = patience  - Romans 5: 3-5

"We can rejoice, too, when we run into problems and trials for we know that they are good for us.  They help us learn to be patient.  And patience develops strength of character in us and helps us trust God more each time we use it until finally our hope and faith are strong and steady."

155

**A candy lifesaver = kindness - 2 Timothy 2: 24**

"The Lord's servant must not quarrel. He must be kind toward all, a good and patient teacher, who is gentle as he corrects his opponents for it may be that God will give them the opportunity to repent and come to know the truth." Or Rev. 2: 19, "I am aware of all your good deeds, your kindness to the poor, your gifts and service to them; also I know your love and faith and patience, and I see your constant improvement in these things."

**A bean = goodness-I Thes. 5: 15**

"See that no one pays back wrong for wrong, but at all times make it your aim to do good to one another and to all people." Or Ps. 34: 15, "For the eyes of the Lord are intently watching all who live good lives, and He gives attention when they cry to Him." Or Ps. 37: 27, "So if you want an external home, leave your evil, low down ways and live good lives." Or II Thes.1:11, "Therefore we also pray always for you that our God would count you worthy of this calling and fulfill all the good pleasure of His goodness ."

**A crown = faithfulness Rev. 2: 1**

"Don't be afraid of anything you are about to suffer, listen! The devil will put you to the test by having some of you thrown into prison, and your troubles will last ten days. Be faithful to me, even if it means death, and I will give you a crown as your prize of victory."

**A lamb = gentleness - Titus 3:2**

"Tell them not to speak evil of anyone, but to be peaceful and friendly and always to show a gentle attitude toward everyone." Or 2 Tim. 2:24, " The Lord's servant must not be quarrelsome; but kindly to everyone, an apt teacher, forbearing, correcting his opponents with gentleness."

**A penny = self-control - Ecc. 1.7: 9**

"Keep your temper under control; it is foolish to harbor a grudge."
Or 2 Peter 1:5-7,  "For this very reason do your best to add  goodness to your faith; to your goodness add knowledge; to your knowledge add self-control; to your self-control add endurance."

**Enjoy finding symbols which are appropriate for your family at a bakery, craft or Bible book store. For example:**
A farmer might use a bean for goodness ( of the earth ) or a penny for self control ( of spending).   A new mom might use a safety pin for faithfulness ( of keeping diapers together); a cotton ball for gentleness and a Hershey's kiss for love ( let the cake cool before inserting it). Peace marches might use candles for Peace. A deep sea diver could use a pearl for patience and a candy lifesaver for kindness.  If you are in Christ, you are a new creature.   May you delight in applying the character trait you selected.

**My Epiphany Gift " by Shirley Halliday Rhodes**

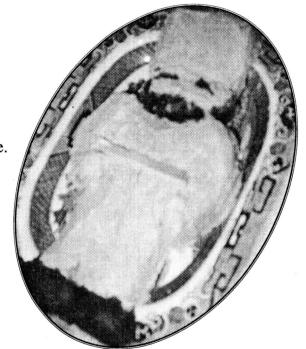

Oh, what will I bring
To my Savior, Priest and King
Nothing less than myself can I give
That He will come into my heart and live.
And then  "O Wondrous Love" I find
Still more gifts to me He gives
That my life may reflect and depart
To others, that not just the Babe, but
My Savior lives in my heart.

157

**King Herod the Great** is the King, in the Christmas story, who ruled Judea from 37-4 BC. He was of Idumean stock rather than Jewish. His marriage to Marianne of the authentic Jewish royal line, (the Hasmonean family) gave him a touch of respectability. Herod grew paranoid his throne when the Wise Men (Matthew 2: 2) inquired, "Where is he who has been born king of the Jews?" This title was reserved for Herod. He was troubled and Jerusalem was filled with rumors (Matthew 2: 3). Herod pretended to want to honor the child and asked the Wise Men to return. In a dream the Wise Men were divinely warned about Herod's plan to murder the child so they did not tell Herod where Jesus was. This enraged Herod and he ordered his soldiers to "kill all the male children in Bethlehem and in all the region who were two years old and under" (Matthew 2: 16). This fulfilled the prophet Jeremiah's words, "A voice was heard in Ramah, wailing and loud lamentation. Rachel weeping for her children; she refused to be consoled because they were no more." Herod had already killed his wife and his three sons earlier. So, it was easy for him to order the deaths of the young innocents (Matthew 2: 18). The nearness of the tomb of Rachel to Bethlehem brought to mind the prophecy from Jer. 31:15. Jesus survived. Joseph was warned in a dream to flee to Egypt.

## HEROD'S THINGS Author Unknown

If, as Herod, we fill our lives with things and again with things.

If we consider ourselves so unimportant that

we must fill every moment of our lives with actions,

when will we have the time to make that long,

slow journey across the desert as did the Magi?

Or sit and watch the sky as did the shepherds?

Or patiently await coming of the Child, as did Mary?

## EPIPHANY TRIVIA

1.  Which two of the four gospels, tell us about the nativity?

2.  Which gospel tells us about the Wise Men?

3.  In what area of Palestine was Bethlehem located?

4.  According to the gospels, how many Wise Men were there ?

5.  According to the gospels, what were their names?

6.  Who decreed that all the world should be taxed ?

7.  The carol, "I Saw Three Ships," tells of three ships sailing into Bethlehem on Christmas Day.   Was it possible for ships to sail into Bethlehem  ?

8.  Where did the Wise Men go after leaving Bethlehem ?

9.  Name the familiar carols whose segments from stanzas are below:

    "But Little Lord Jesus no crying He Makes," and

    "O Morning Stars, together proclaim His Holy Birth."

10. What is the best translation of a Bible for your children?


ANSWERS: 1. Matthew & Luke; 2. Matthew; 3. Southern-Judea; 4. No number given; 5. Names not given; 6. Caesar Augustus; 7. No wooden ships, however, camels are called "Ships of the Desert"; 8. To their own land; 9. "Away in the Manger" & "Little Town of Bethlehem"; 10.  My pastor says that the answer is you!!  You are translating it into life for them to understand.


As you put things away think how you honored Jesus on His birth.  Did you make room for Him in your Inn or was He in the stable ?   Buy a Nativity set on sale.  It will make great wedding gift.  It is something that will remind the couple of Jesus for the rest of their Christmases.  Start a tradition of giving everyone in the Sunday School one figure each year.

159

# CHAPTER 14

## MESSENGERS FROM GOD

### Angels We have Heard on High

Angel is the translation of a Hebrew word meaning messenger. Angels have three purposes: to **bring messages** from God to mankind; to **carry out tasks** on earth for God while acting as our guardians; **to worship and glorify God.**

**Angels as messengers** appeared in the Christmas story six times. First Gabriel appeared to Zachariah then to Mary. Next, an angel appeared in a dream to Joseph. One angel appeared to the shepherds followed by a multitude of heavenly host (Luke 2:10-14). Finally, an angel warned the Wise Men not to go back to Herod and told Joseph to flee to Egypt. Angels have intelligence. See Dan. 9 : 21-22, Dan. 10: 14, Rev 19: 10 and Rev. 19:10. In the Old Testament Jacob's message was received through a dream." And he dreamed a staircase reached from earth to heaven, and he saw the angels of God going up and down upon it." Jacob wrestled with one of the angels (Genesis 28: 12). One brought visions to Ezekiel. Angels report directly to God (Job 2:1).

**Angels carrying out tasks** can help humans (Hebrews 1:14 ). Angels will join all believers in the heavenly kingdom ( Hebrews 12: 22-23). Some people believe angels minister to the believer at the moment of death and lead the soul to Heaven ( Luke 16: 22 ).

**Angels are caregivers and guardians** "The angels of the Lord guard and rescue all who reverence God" (Ps. 34:7 ). " To his angels God has given command about you, that they guard you in all your ways. Upon their hands they will bear you up, lest you dash your foot against a stone " (Psalm 91:11-12). In Gen. 3: 24, where angels first appear, they were stationed at the door of paradise to guard the Garden of Eden. In the New England Primer Dr. Watt's Cradle Hymn told children about angels guarding their bed at night and watching over Jesus at his birth. He may have gotten his idea from Genesis 28:12, Psalm 34: 7 and Kings 6:17 where angels encamped around those that feared God. Angels are innumerable ( Psalm 68:17, Daniel 7: 9 -10, Matthew 26: 53, Hebrews 1: 22, and Revelations 5: 11). Catholics believe, they receive at birth a companion that fits their personality. Ancient Jewish angelology also taught the personal-angel theory. The Talmud speaks of every Jew being assigned eleven thousand guardian angels at birth. Protestants believe they shouldn't pray to angels but can ask angels to intervene for them. Angels, acting alone or in great gatherings, formed a heavenly court playing crucial roles especially in the Jewish Torah and other Old Testament books.

**Angels glorify God.** Luke 2:13 says " Suddenly there was with the angel a multitude of the heavenly host praising God and saying,' Glory to God in the highest and on earth peace among men with whom he is pleased.' "

**Angels have a hierarchy.** The New Testament suggests **Archangels** were at the top. Christian and Jewish writings varied on how many archangels there were but finally it became seven because of Revelation 8:2 and Colossians1: 17. tell the angels will pronounce the seven trumpet judgments, made by Christ. **Seraphim** are mentioned in just one passage (Is. 6: 2-3). **Cherub** is singular of Cherubim, the warrior angels. In Solomon's Temple, there were carved Cherubim thirty feet high. Their wings were fifteen feet wide. Paul mentions five groups of angels: virtues, principalities, powers, dominions, and thrones. The book of Hebrew, tells us why Jesus is higher than the angels.

**Angels have names.** Michael, the archangel is mentioned in Dan.10:13, 21, Dan.12 :1, Jude 9, and Rev.12:7. Gabriel appears four times in the Bible. His name in Hebrew means "hero of God" In Daniel 8:16 and 9:21 he is described as "swift in flight. "In the Christmas story, he is God's messenger. The Apocryphal lists two angels, Raphael and Uriel.

**Humans can not become angels** although people often refer to innocent children as angels like in Dixie Schaefer's poem "To An Angel." Angels were created by God ( Gen.2:1, Neh.9:6, Eph.3: 9 ). They were present at the creation of the world. They are created to live forever (Rev. 4: 8). Angels do not marry (Matthew 22: 30). They are spirit beings ( Hebrews 1: 7, 12, 14, and Psalm 104: 4 ). Angels can take on human form to conceal their true identity to those to whom they are sent. They are invisible beings ( Romans 1: 18-32, Colossians 2: 18, Revelation 19: 10 and 22: 9 ).

**Angels can be good and bad.** Angels can harm people ( Mark 5:15 ). After the Babylonian exile, the Jews developed the idea of good versus bad angels. In the New Testament in Revelation there is a battle between the bad angels lead by Satan and the good angels. They possess wills (Isaiah 14:12 to 15 and Jude 6 ). They also display joy ( Job 38: 7 and Luke 2: 13).

**Angels in art** began to appear in the fourth century, the artist gave them wings to distinguish them from the apostles or other holy men. My Precious Moment Angels are "too sweet" but I enjoy them. However, if I had known more about angels when I bought them, I would have gotten ones that showed strength like Gabriel and Michael. It is difficult to find angels like the ones depicted in the Bible. Most angels we see on Christmas trees do not represent the angels of the Bible but the world's view. We found Gabriel made by Seraphim. He still is a wimp compared to the Bible angels who are virile!

House above is Joseph's house with his father Jacob. Mary's house is below, where David is placing the angel by Mary to tell her the news from God.

# GLOSSARY

## YOU CAN'T GIVE AWAY WHAT YOU DON'T KNOW

ABIDING:   Staying near a place or person for a long time.

ADVENT:   Means coming. It is the season before Christmas, lasting four weeks.

ADVENT CALENDAR:   It can be made of cardboard and other materials to look like a little house.   It's constructed with twenty-five  windows.   Each day one is opened to find an appropriate Scripture verse or symbol for that day.   It helps a child keep track of how many days are left until Christmas.

ANGEL:   A Hebrew word meaning a messenger.   Read the Chapter on Angels.

ANNA:   Means favor or grace.   Prophets like Anna (Luke 2: 36) were known for their spiritual wisdom and proclamation of God's word to the people. Along with Simeon, she helped testify to Jesus as God's Redeemer.   Her testimony, as a woman, would not have been very important in the Jewish Courts of the day.   But Luke puts her in his gospel, probably to show one of the changes Jesus wanted to bring to His followers.   No longer should they regard women as untrustworthy witnesses, but they should be full members of a new community of faith in Jesus.   The verses tell us she spent her time in the temple serving God through fasting and praying.   No doubt her prayers expressed a longing for God's Anointed to come.   Her years of hearing the scriptures read regularly apparently gave her a discerning knowledge.

ARK OF THE COVENANT: A receptacle for the Ten Commandments and other holy relics of Israel's faith. They were the main part of God's covenant with the people of Israel. The Ark, a sign of divine presence symbolized by it's lid of solid gold with two golden cherubim, was called the mercy seat. It was also called "the ark of the covenant of the Lord of hosts, who is enthroned on the cherubim." The Ark was built of acacia wood. It was 45 by 27 inches. The Israelites carried it until the temple was built, on gilded poles inserted through rings. Then after the destruction of the temple no one knows what happened to it. After they rebuilt the temple, the Holy of Holies was kept in darkness since the Ark, God's light was lost.

BARREN: A woman not giving birth to a child. She was considered cursed if she didn't have children to carry on the family line and inherit the property.

BEHOLD: Look ! See !

BELLS: Metal which rings when struck. Before newspapers, church bells were rung to announce special events, news and a call to worship. On Christmas Eve and Day, they announced the birthday of Jesus. Some people believe the devil is sent scamping by the joyous sound of bells. The ancient Hebrews' high priest wore robes with tiny golden bells on the bottom of their hems.

BENEDICTUS :Latin for" Blessed", the first word in the oracle of Luke 1: 68-79.

BETROTHAL: An official relationship in which two people promise to marry each other, usually occurring at a very early age. An agreement with more legal weight than a wedding. It was arranged by the groom's father whose duty was to make the best arrangement for his child. He chose the bride, mainly from the groom's own clan. Sometimes, the girl was only twelve years old. Mary was probably very young. It was a covenant between two families. After he chose a wife, he had to negotiate the amount of the mohar. Fifty shekels of silver was the common rate. The marriage agreement completed, the couple were betrothed in a formal ceremony in front of witnesses. The groom and his father paid the mohar. The bride's father gave his assent, saying, "as Saul told David, you now are my son-in-law." This ritual was usually twelve months before the wedding. Now they were considered husband and wife. The betrothal could only be broken by a divorce. If the groom died the bride was considered a widow. A child born during this time would have been legitimate. Hence, Matthew calls Mary and Joseph husband and wife.

CAESAR AUGUSTUS: The Roman Emperor who decreed a census to be taken. The name of Caesar means kingly. His edict in Luke 2: 1 was to have people enroll in the place of origin of their family. It was to make collecting taxes easier by having their names on the rolls. This decree provided the event for Jesus to fulfill the prophecy the Messiah would come out of Bethlehem.

CANDY CANES: Made by a candy maker as a reminder and witness of Jesus' birth, ministry and death. . He began with a stick of pure white to symbolize the Virgin Birth and the sinless nature of Jesus. He made it in the shape of the shepherd's staff. Upside down it becomes the "J "for the precious name of Jesus. The three small stripes show the marks of the scourging Jesus received. The large red stripe was for the blood shed by Christ on the cross. It is made of hard candy to symbolize the solid rock, the foundation of the Church and the firmness of the promises of God.

CARPENTER: A carpenter worked with wood, metal and stone and hand tools, such as the axe and hatchet as in Deut. 19: 5, Ps. 74: 6, the hammer in Judg. 4: 21, the saw in Is.10: 15, the plumb line, ruler, plane and compass in Is. 44:13 and Zech. 2:1. His main tools were a stone hammer, mallet, shaver, chisel, bow drill, an iron saw (size of a large knife),, and sandstone for smoothing. He made yokes for oxen, threshing boards, winnowing forks, wooden plows and other things for farmers. He made benches, chairs, beds, boxes, coffins and carts. Those that lived by the sea made boats. The carpenter, in a small place like Nazareth, made small carved items for parts of houses. Most homes were made with stone or mud-brick walls, but he would put in place the wooden beams and support for roof structures. He worked on large public buildings and synagogues. He often had a little workshop opened to the street. His family lived behind it or above it. The best known carpenters in the Bible were Noah (Gen. 6 ), Jesus and Joseph (Mark 6: 3).

CAVE: A natural or hollow place in the earth due to the presence of chalk, limestone and sandstone formations. Some are massive in size. Natural caves are in abundance in Palestine. The tradition is Jesus was born in a cave.

CENSUS TAKER: A person who took an official count of the population. This unpopular job was associated with tax collection. A census was mentioned in the Bible in connection with Moses, David, Solomon and the Romans.

CHERUB: A heavenly being. Plural is cherubim.

CHRISTIAN TORAH: It was a manual for Christian discipleship, organized in a way to resemble and serve as the Pentateuch ( 5 books in the Torah).

Matthew's gospel has five major speeches of Jesus, taken together they give us a five-volume "Christian Torah." They are:

5:1-7: 27   Sermon on the Mount given to a large crowd.

9:35- 10:42   Instructions given to the twelve chosen by Christ.

13:1-52 Parables of the Kingdom given on a crowded beach.

18:1-35   Instructions on community given to the disciples.

24: 1, -25: 46 The Olivet Discourse given to the disciples (Final exam)


CIRCUMCISION: The cutting off the foreskin of the penis. It was a physical sign of the covenant between God and man. It was replaced with baptism in the Christian home.


CRECHE : A Nativity scene. It shows figures of Mary, Joseph, Jesus, Wise Men, shepherds and various animals.


DECREE : An order from someone in power.


DOVE: A small pigeon (Lev. 12: 8) prescribed as the offering to purify the mother after childbirth, if the family couldn't afford a lamb.


DREAM : An experiences when a person is asleep. A vision happens when a person is awake. Both are used by God to communicate His will to the people. An angel appeared to Joseph in a dream before and after the birth of Jesus. The Wise Men from the East in Matthew's account, were warned in a dream not to return to tell Herod about Jesus. In a waking vision, an angel appeared to Mary to tell her she would give birth to the Son of God. Dreams and visions are treated as almost identical.

EGYPT: A country in NE Africa. Jesus going to Egypt fulfilled the scriptures. The cry, "Out of Egypt have I called my Son," is in Hos. 11:1. It is a reference to the deliverance of the nation Israel from its period of slavery in Egypt. When Jesus comes out of Egypt, there is a feeling Jesus' life is the epitome of the story of Israel and the experience of each Christian. Sometimes, we stay in "Egypt" too long and don't move on to the higher goal God has for us. Mary and Joseph going to Egypt and back seems to be a parallel between the Old and New Testament.

ELIZABETH: Zachariah's wife who prophesied the Lord would be born of Mary.

EPIPHANY: A visit of a King to his people. This is from the Greek word meaning manifest, appear or show. The Feast of Epiphany is celebrated on January 6th, after the twelve days of Christmas. It is also called Wise Men's day since this is the day Jesus' appearance to the Magi manifested to the Gentile world Jesus the Messiah was born. Read the Epiphany Chapter.

FORERUNNER : A messenger or person sent ahead to tell of the coming of someone special. John the Baptist was the forerunner of Jesus.

FRANKINCENSE : A sweet fragrant gum resin containing so much oil it could be burned. It exuded in large, light yellowish-brown tears from Boswellis trees which grow in South Arabia, Ethiopia and India. A gift, from the Wise Men to Jesus, fit for a high priest.

GABRIEL: The angel in the Christmas story who made the announcement to both Mary and to Zachariah. One of the four angels given a name in the Bible.

169

GALILEE : A region of northern Palestine. It includes Nazareth and Nain

GENEALOGY: A recorded history of one's ancestry. Luke traces the genealogy of Jesus back to Adam, father of the human race. This is a spiritual genealogy since it connects His bloodline to God. Therefore, Luke includes the genealogy after Jesus' baptism. Luke was a Gentile and his gospel highlights Gentiles. Luke makes Mary the central figure. Some feel he heard the story from Mary. Matthew traces Jesus' genealogy back to Abraham, father of the Jews, from the perspective of Joseph. We know Joseph was only the earthly father; however, the genealogy had to conform to Hebrew usage. It placed Jesus in the legal line of the king promised to God's people. Through Joseph, the line from David continued. It gave a reason for Jesus to be born in Bethlehem. Matthew links Jesus to the royal house of David and to the patriarch Abraham, which makes Jesus heir to God's promises and the fulfillment of the divine plan for mankind. Since Mary was from Galilee, it would have been hard to fulfill the prophesy that the Messiah would be born in Bethlehem. God used an Emperor to have Mary and Joseph go to Bethlehem. Matthew included four women in the genealogy who were sinners and foreigners. Matthew includes Gentiles and Patriarchs. Jesus is a mixer of classes. All are one in Him.

GENTILE: A person who is a non-Jew. There was an inscription forbidding Gentiles from entering the Temple in Jerusalem posted in the court yard.

GOLD : A precious metal named in the Bible 385 times.

HALO: The circle above an angel's head is a halo or nimbus, an aura of light and glory, just as the message of Jesus birth is one of light and glory.

HANUKKAH: Hebrew for " dedication". The eight-day festival commemorating the rededication of the temple in Jerusalem by Judas Maccabeus in 164 B.C. The story is told in 1 and 2 Maccabees. The temple had to be purified because it had been used to worship Zeus and swine flesh had been on the altar. Jews feel pigs are unfit to eat. There was only enough oil for purifying it one day but the oil, by a miracle, lasted for eight. Now on Hanukkah, Jewish people light eight candles in a Menorah with the ninth candle called the shamash, or the servant candle, they light one candle each night until all eight are burning. Hanukkah is also known as Feast of the Lights (because of the oil that burned for eight days) and Feast of Dedication, or Feast of the Maccabees.

HARBINGER: It means Messenger.

HARLOT: A prostitute. One, named Rahab, changed her lifestyle and was praised in Heb.11:31.

HEROD: The King who ruled from 37 to 4 BC. Read Epiphany Chapter.

HOLLY AND IVY: These plants are symbols for the promise of eternal life. Called the holy tree, the pointed leaves resemble the crown of thorns put on Jesus when He was crucified. The red berries look like drops of blood.

HOLY OF HOLIES: A cubical room thirty feet long within the temple. It was called the inner sanctuary, most holy oracle, shrine or debhir (which is Hebrew). It had three gold walls and a thick curtain on one side. Behind this veil was the Ark of the Covenant. Only on the day of Atonement, which was once a year, could the high priest enter the darkness to gain forgiveness.

171

The room was left dark after the ark was lost ( in the Babylonian conquest).

HORN OF SALVATION: Means "a mighty savior."  A horn was often a metaphor in  the Old Testament meaning "power". It was a symbolic way of referring to the power of God (I Sam 2:10). In Advent many people decorate with horns as a reminder Jesus, the horn of Salvation,  is coming.

IMMANUEL : Hebrew for "God is with us."   Jesus is identified as Immanuel.

INCARNATION: A term meaning "to enter into or become flesh."   It is the Christian doctrine which states the Son of Man preexisted and became man in Jesus.  This word is not in the NT, but the development of it is.  In Hebrews1:1 to 3 the notion of preexistence is clear.  John 1:1-17  proclaims the pre-existence of the word of God,  "The word became flesh and dwelt among us."

INCENSE:  The perfume or smoke which comes from a compound of aromatic gums and spices as they burn.  The ingredients were made by skilled perfum-ers ( Exod. 37: 29 and 30: 34 ).  The burning of incense aids in atonement and adds a pleasant odor to the priestly material and the animal sacrifices (Lev.1: 15-16).  It is also linked to prayer (Luke 1: 10,  Rev. 5: 8  and  8: 3-4 ).

INN: A hotel or building where a person could eat or sleep. These were often large private dwellings (Luke 2:7 ).  Christians were encouraged to open their homes to strangers since some inns were run by dishonest innkeepers.

INNKEEPER: A person who managed an inn in Jesus' day. (Luke 10:34).

JESSE TREE: Jesse, the father of David, is represented as a tree. Judgment upon Israel cut down the tree. The judgment was not final, for the stump was to produce a new shoot. Thus God's covenant with David is fulfilled with Christ. The Jesse tree is a symbol of the lineage of Jesus Christ. See in Chapter Four.

JESUS: Means "Jehovah saves," "He will deliver His people from their sins" and "the Lord is Salvation." Salvation means delivered from sins. Y'shua is Jesus' Jewish name.

JOHN: Means, "God's gracious gift." Gabriel, said he would be filled with the Holy Spirit from birth. John is the forerunner of the Messiah promised in the Old Testament, in Mal. 3:16. A prophetic utterance was heard after four hundred years of silence.

JUDEA : The whole area of Palestine.

KINSMAN: Relative of the same family. Elizabeth was kinsman to Mary.

LIGHT: Symbolizes the idea of God's revelation (Is a. 9: 2). The light the shepherds saw was symbolic of divine revelation. That is why the message was accepted as the word of God. Simeon said Jesus would be a light to the Gentiles. Many people put lights up at Christmas to remind us Jesus said, "I am the light of the world," He said, "Who ever follows me will never walk in darkness, but will have the light of life." Jesus can brighten our lives more than any Christmas tree lights or Hanukkah Menorah.

173

LINE OF DAVID: Relatives which followed after David. Among the Jews, women usually married within the same clan (Numbers 27 :1-11). Both Mary and Joseph were of the house of David. However, the Jewish law felt it was binding if it was passed on by the male. Therefore, Joseph was important.

MAGI: See Wise Men.

MAGNIFICAT : The song Mary happily sang, about the blessing which God had bestowed upon her (Luke 1: 39-56). She did it under the inspiration of the Holy Spirit, but she used words familiar to her thru the Scripture. This song is similar to Hannah's song of praise given under similar circumstances in 1 Sam. 2:1-10. The name comes from the first word in the Latin version.

MANGER: A trough to hold hay for animals. Jesus was placed in one at birth.

MELCHIZEDEK: Priest of the most High God. In Ezra 2: 59-62, he is described as having neither beginning of days nor end of life. He suddenly emerged from the unknown and as suddenly disappeared. He is a type of undying priesthood. In Hebrews, it shows how great a personage he was. Even Abraham (and through him virtually Levi) paid tithes, thus showing Melchizedek was superior. Jesus was made a high priest after the order of Melchizedek, a higher office than the Aaronic priesthood.

MENORAH: A golden candelabrum placed in the holy room, adjoining the holy of holies, in the temple's interior. It held nine candles. Eight candles for the eight days of Hanukkah and a servant candle ( shamash)  to light the others.

MESSIAH: Means anointed, since leaders were anointed with oil. In the Old Testament people prayed for a Messiah, the expected savior and deliverer of the Hebrew people. They looked for a Messiah who would not die. There were prophecies about him. In the New Testament, Jesus is the Messiah who fulfilled all the prophecies of the Old Testament.

MYRRH: An oil used to embalm dead bodies ( Mark15: 23; John 19:39).

NAZARETH: This is a place where Jesus lived thus fulfilling the prophecy referring to Nazareth: "He shall be called a Nazarene." Nazareth means shoot or branch, as in Is a.11:1. Jesus is from the shoot or stem of Jesse.

NAZARITE: To be a Nazarite was voluntary, but John was one from birth. It was a symbol of holiness. Chapter Six in Numbers discloses a Nazarite could not drink alcohol use any razor or participate in any ceremonial defilement.

NUNC DIMITTIS :Latin for the opening words Simeon says in Luke 2 :29. " Lord, now let thy servant depart in peace, according to thy word. For my eyes have seen thy salvation." This prayer is used in many churches.

PALESTINE : A region of 8,000 square miles on the eastern edge of the domain of Rome. Millions of Jews (mainly tax-paying units) lived there..

POINSETTIA: A plant shaped like the star of Bethlehem. Dr. Joel Poinsett, our first ambassador to Mexico, saw it and brought it back to United States.

PRIESTS: Holy men who served mainly at an altar. The English word priest is a shortening of the Greek title "presbyter," which means elder. The Hebrew word is Cohen. It is derived from a Hebrew word meaning to stand, since it was customary for a priest to stand before God in religious rites. They wore nothing on their feet. Only bare feet could touch the temple's holy ground.

PROPHECY: A prediction of something to come. Initiated by God, who gives his message to people through a prophet or some chosen messenger. The Hebrew was given increased authority and was seen as the carrier of God's word. Prophecies about the Messiah were fulfilled after four thousand years. After Jesus came prophecies declined. Read the Chapter Nine on prophecies.

PURIFICATION: This ceremony is described in Lev. 12: 2. The mother is considered unclean for seven days after the birth of her son. On the eighth day he is circumcised. Counting from that day, the mother is to remain separate, thirty-three days longer. At the end of that time, or forty days from the birth, she is to offer a sacrifice consisting of a lamb or, if poor, a pair of doves.

SACRIFICE: An offering to God, usually made at an altar. In the days of Jesus, doves, sheep and cattle were often sacrificed to God.

SAVIOR : A person who saves others from danger or death. The title applied to Jesus by Christians because he saves them from eternal death.

SCRIBES : Government officials or others who could read and write. They kept records, wrote letters, copied documents, and studied the Hebrew Scriptures. Hence, their role took on a religious meaning.

When Jesus was born, scribes were interpreters of the law and professional Torah scholars , both oral and written. They made up a large segment of the Sanhedrin (Judaism's highest court). Many held offices in the synagogues and local judicial bodies. Some belonged to the Sadducees or the Pharisees. The scribes pointed to Micah 5: 2 saying the Messiah would be born in Bethlehem.

SCRIPTURE: Sacred writings; the Bible. When the New Testament talks about the Scriptures, it means the Old Testament. Jewish Bibles do not contain the New Testament. In Christian Bibles the Old Testament is put together in a different order. The Prophets are placed last so the final verse of Malachi points to the forerunner of Jesus. "Behold, I will send you Elijah the prophet." Scriptures mean both the Old and New Testament to Christians.

SHEPHERD: A man who tends and guards sheep. Shepherding was a major occupation in Palestine. Shepherds tended sheep and goats; were breeders and shearers. Shepherds were a metaphor for spiritual direction and leadership. In the Old Testament, God is often called a Shepherd, (Ps. 23, Is. 40:11). The flocks reserved for the temple sacrifices were kept in the field near Bethlehem throughout the year.

SIMEON : Means, "one who hears and obeys." In Luke 2: 25-27, we see Simeon's blessing was not his own, but came from the Holy Spirit. It is mentioned three times. His praise is full of reference to the prophecies of the Old Testament. Simeon knew God would show him the Redeemer. He knew to look for a baby and not a political leader. In Luke 2: 29-31, Simeon tells the international significance of Jesus. He came for both Gentile and Jew. He is presented to his own people in the form laid down by the Jewish law.

**SWADDLING CLOTHES** : Strips of fabric four or five inches wide and several yards long. Some ethnic groups still wash and rub salt on the baby and then bind them with cloth. Newborns "swaddled" or wrapped snugly in cloth for several months tend to have strong and straight bones. Jesus the Word came wrapped in swaddling cloth.

**SYNAGOGUE** : The building which Jews use for meetings, study and worship.

**TEMPLE** : A building dedicated to worship. The temple was sacred because an angel had shown David where to build it. Gentiles could be killed for entering certain parts of it. Solomon built the first permanent temple of the Lord. Up to that time it had been a movable tabernacle. Solomon's temple was razed and the furnishing taken off to Babylon, in 587. Jews built a second temple in 520. Then Herod tore it down to erect his own monument. The Romans in A.D. 70 destroyed it.

**TORAH** :The Books of Moses and the Pentateuch, which means five scrolls of instruction or law. The five scrolls (Books of Moses) are Genesis, Exodus, Leviticus, Numbers, and Deuteronomy. Moses warned the people to carefully observe all the words of law. The English word "law" does not convey all Moses intended. Both the hearing and the doing of the law made the Torah. It was a manner of life, a way to live based on the covenant God made with His people. See Christian Torah.

**TWELFTH NIGHT:** It is the last night of Christmas and the evening preceding Epiphany. There are twelve days and twelve nights of Christmas.

TWELVE DAY OF CHRISTMAS: They occurs from December 25th to January 5th. Twelve days of Christmas," was written in secret code when Christians were not supposed to practice their religion. Read Chapter 12 and learn the code.

VIRGIN BIRTH : The male part of the conception of Jesus was taken over by the Holy Spirit of God. The earliest inference to the virgin birth is in Genesis 3:15, in the first announcement of the deliverer who would come. It said he'd be the offspring of "a woman". A male parent is not mentioned. In Isaiah 7:14 a prophecy spoken to Ahaz says a virgin would conceive and bear a son and his name would be called Immanuel, which is "God with us." Miraculously, Mary was overshadowed by the Holy Spirit. Matthew endorses the virgin birth by using a Greek term that means virgin, one who has never had intercourse with a male. Matthew tells us Jesus was born without a human father.

WISE MEN : Experts in astrology who studied the stars. They expected a special star to fulfill prophecies of Balaam and Daniel. Read page 152.

WREATH : A circle of evergreens showing God is everlasting. God has no beginning and no end. God is the Alpha and the Omega (Greek letters A and Z).

XMAS :The word Xmas started in the early church. In Greek, X is the first letter of Christ's name. The Greek name for Christ translated into the Roman alphabet as Khritos. The first two letters in Kristos are chi and rho and can be written XP as Christ's monogram. Xmas has been used since the fourteenth century. Christmas has been used since 1038. Christmas comes from the word Cristes Maesse, an English phrase meaning the Mass of Christ.

For additional copies print the following information below for shipping:

Name.....................................................................................................

Address.................................................................................................

City, State, Zip.....................................................................................

Phone....................................................................................................

_____ copies of Make Room For Jesus in Your Inn @ 15.= $_____

Postage and Handling @ 1.50 per book _____ $_____

Michigan Sales Tax 6%_____= $_____

Total =

For a Church Fund Raiser order 30 or more with advance order forms. Send:

Name.....................................................................................................

Address.................................................................................................

City, State, Zip.....................................................................................

Phone....................................................................................................

_____copies of Make Room For Jesus in Your Inn @12.50 = $_____

Postage and Handling @ 1.50 per book (no charge for pick up)  $_____

Michigan Sales Tax 6%_____= $_____

Total =

Send check and order to:

Make Room for Jesus

 % Gwen Bancroft

558 Bay East Dr.,

Traverse City,  MI 49686

Phone  number:  1-231-929-9327

e Mail: bMercier@Prodigy.net